Mel Bay Presents

# A Guide to Non-Jazz Improvisation

## By Dick Weissman & Dan Fox

**Fiddle Edition**

## CD contents

| | | | |
|---|---|---|---|
| 1 | Tuning [1:09] | 12 | Cajun [1:06] |
| 2 | Melody, slides & grace notes [4:08] | 13 | Irish [4:14] |
| 3 | Neighbor notes & passing tones [5:28] | 14 | American Folk [3:41] |
| 4 | Slides & tremolo [1:31] | 15 | Ragtime [3:30] |
| 5 | Scales [4:46] | 16 | Gospel [0:55] |
| 6 | Modes [8:44] | 17 | Blues & Boogie [2:06] |
| 7 | Specialty scales [4:45] | 18 | Odd meters [3:32] |
| 8 | Double Stops [3:27] | 19 | International [8:40] |
| 9 | Black Eyed Susie & Arpeggios [1:34] | 20 | Rock and roll [1:40] |
| 10 | Country & Western [4:26] | 21 | A Tuning [5:32] |
| 11 | Bluegrass [3:30] | | |

*Note: This CD contains more than one example on each track.*

1 2 3 4 5 6 7 8 9 0

© 2007 BY MEL BAY PUBLICATIONS, INC., PACIFIC, MO 63069.

*Visit us on the Web at www.melbay.com — E-mail us at email@melbay.com*

# Table of Contents

Foreword ..............................................4

What you should know
    before starting this book .........................5

**PART 1–TECHNIQUES OF IMPROVISATION**

Getting started ...........................................6
Grace notes ...............................................7
Double, triple and quadruple grace notes..9
Mordents, turns, and trills ...........................10
Neighbor notes, upper and lower
    neighbor notes .....................................11
Passing tones, diatonic ...............................13
Passing tones, chromatic.............................14
Slides......................................................15
Tremolo ..................................................16
Improvising with Melodies (Summing up) ..18
A Bit of Music Theory ................................19
Major scales ............................................20
Improvising with major scales .....................23
Jingle Bells ...............................................24
Minor scales; harmonic minor scales ..........25
Improvising with harmonic minor scales ....27
Melodic minor scales .................................28
Improvising with melodic minor scales ......29
Improvising with modes .............................30
Ionian mode; Ionian Item ..........................31
Dorian mode; The Drunken Sailor...............32
Phrygian mode; The Spanish Tinge ............33
Lydian mode; Lydia's Lunch .......................34
Mixolydian Mode; Old Joe Clark ...............35
Aeolian mode; Shady Grove ......................36
Locrian mode; Transposing modes ............37
Specialty scales; D minor hexachord;
    Pretty Polly.........................................38
Pentatonic scale on F;
    Oh Susanna (part 1) ............................39
Pentatonic scale on C; Shortnin' Bread ....40
Tetrachord; In the Pines .............................41
Double stops .............................................42
Improvising with double stops;
    Just Lopin' Along ................................43
Double stops: The Missouri Waltz.................44

Using an open string as a drone;
    Black-Eyed Susie..................................45
Improvising with Chords..............................46
Common major chords ..............................47
Common minor chords ..............................48
Common seventh chords ...........................49
Improvising with chords .............................50

**PART 2—TUNES AND STYLES**

**Country and Western**
Bury Me Not on the Lone Prairie.................52
Railroad Bill ..............................................53
Country waltz: Beautiful Brown Eyes .........54

**Bluegrass Fiddle**
The Eighth of January ...............................56
Hammering on ........................................57
Little Maggie ............................................58
John Hardy ..............................................60
Banks of the Ohio.....................................62

**Cajun Music**
Pardon My French ....................................64

**Celtic (Irish) Music**
The Irish Washerwoman ..............................66
Straight Jig................................................67
Danny Boy................................................69

**American Folk Music**
Wildwood Flower ......................................71
Sweet Betsy From Pike ...............................73
Fly Around, My Pretty Little Miss ................75

**Ragtime**
Temptation Rag ........................................77

**Gospel**
White Gospel: Will the Circle Be Unbroken 79
Black Gospel: Wade in the Water .............80

**The Blues**
Blues progressions .....................................81

Blues scales .............................................82
*Blues in C* .............................................83
*Pizzicato Boogie* .....................................84
Pitch bending .........................................85
*Rockin' the Blues* ...................................86

### Odd Meters
5/4, 7/8, 9/8 ...........................................87
*Five Times Four* .....................................88
*The Other Bela* ......................................89
*Odyssey in 9/8* .......................................90

### Exotic scales
Whole tone scale ....................................91
Klezmer Music; Misherabach:
    *Chosen Kalle Mazel Tov* ................92
Klezmer Music: Harmonic minor:
    *Havah Nagilah* .............................94
Fralgish or Greek scale:
    *Goodbye to Piraeus* .....................96
Gypsy scale: *Gypsy Fantasy* .................97
Gypsy scale: *At the Gypsy Caravan* .........98
Scottish music: *Highland Fling* .............99
Rumanian music: *Horra* ...................100
Palestinian music: *Artsa Alinu* ...........101
Japanese scale: *The Geisha's Lament;*
    Chinese scale: *The Golden Bell* ...........102

### Rock and Roll
The I VI II V progression in C .............103
The I VI II V progression in G .............104
*Back to the Fifties* ...............................105
The boogaloo or a cute-time feel............106

### Disco
*Disco Daze...* .......................................107

### Country and Folk Rock
*Nevada Motels* ....................................108

### The A tuning
*Rye Whiskey* .......................................109
*Lost Indian* ..........................................110
*Sally Goodin'* ......................................111
*Amazing Grace* ..................................112

Playing with other people .....................113
Planning your arrangements..................113
Developing an original style .................113

Fiddle Books of Interest .........................114
Fiddle Recordings of Interest..................115

Dick Weissman .......................................116
Dan Fox ................................................116

# Foreword

The violin is the most versatile and expressive instrument known in western classical music. This book is devoted to exploring other aspects of this beautiful instrument, popularly known as the fiddle. Whether playing a blazing bluegrass solo, a sentimental country ballad, a ragtime piece, or a folk song, the violin speaks out in its own unique voice.

This book is about improvisation... everything from putting a few decorative embellishments on a pre-existing melody to a free fantasy that uses the melody and chord progression as springboards for the player's creativity.

If you haven't improvised before, you can use this book as a road map to coming up with new and inventive solos. If you're used to improvising but don't know how you're doing it, or wish you could do it better, this book will help you on your way. In Part 1 you'll learn the basic techniques of improvising: embellishments, passing tones, slides, trills, major and minor scales, modes, hexachords, pentatonic scales, tetrachords, double stops, drones and chords. In Part 2, you'll learn great tunes and how to play variations on them. Various styles are discussed and illustrated: Country and Western, Bluegrass, Cajun, Irish (Celtic), American Folk, Ragtime, Gospel, and Blues. In the next section you'll learn about odd meters such as 5/4 and 7/8, and exotic scales like the whole tone scale, as well as scales from other cultures—Gypsy, Japanese, Chinese, Jewish, Greek, etc. Then comes a section on Rock music followed by a discussion of unusual tunings with many practical examples. The final section discusses such subjects as Playing with Other People, Developing an Original Style, and Recommended Books and Recordings.

It's our hope that this book will provide you with fertile ideas that will free you from the straitjacket of a particular style. There's a great deal of wonderful music out there, and learning to play as much of it as you can is a worthy and attainable goal.

Dan Fox and Dick Weissman

## What You Should Know Before Starting This Book

1. How to tune your violin

2. The notes in the open position. In the open position, all four open strings are used in addition to the four fingers of the left hand. For the ordinary fingering of every note in the open position, see below.

3. The basic rhythms in 4/4, 3/4, 2/4, and 6/8 time.

4. Ordinary bowings.

The notes in the open position using sharps

0  1  1  1  2  3  3  4    0  1  1  2    2  3  3  4    0  1  1  2    2  3  3  4    0  1  1  2    2  3  3  4

The notes in the open position using flats

4  4  3  3  2  2  1  0    4  4  3  3  2  1  1  0    4  4  3  3  2  1  1  0    4  4  3  2  2  1  1  0

Important note: In the open position the notes D, A, and E can be played open or on the next lower string with the 4th finger. In actual playing situations you should ordinarily choose the fingering that is easier, but there are other considerations also. More about this later in the book.

5. You can assume that all the music in this book is played in the open position unless otherwise noted. Later in the book we sometimes use higher positions. As is traditional, these will be indicated with Roman numerals. I=1st position, II=2nd position, V=5th position, etc.

### Optional but highly recommended

All of us have a tendency to play faster when the music is easy and slower when it's more difficult. In order to combat this tendency and keep a steady beat, we highly recommend using a **metronome**. This device produces a steady stream of clicks as slow as 40 beats and as fast as 208 beats per minute. Modern metronomes are electronic* and are very reasonable in cost; a reliable one can be purchased for as little as $20. Many models can be set to any meter (2/4, 3/4, 4/4 etc.), marking the first beat of each measure with a loud click. Some models also produce the note A=440 which is a great help in keeping your violin at the proper pitch. Most of the pieces in this book have a marking such as MM=80. This means that your goal is to play the piece at 80 beats per minute.

*Old-fashioned metronomes were mechanical and worked on the pendulum principle. We don't recommend them because a) They have to be rewound fairly often, b) unless they are placed on a perfectly level surface, the beats will be unequal and c) they cannot be set to an exact number of beats per minute, so it's more difficult to measure your progress.

### What is Improvisation?

Improvisation means anything from adding a few decorative touches to an existing melody to completely free improvisation that has no rules or guidelines and relies totally on the player's instinct.

### What's so good about improvising?

Improvisation is a way to express your own musical personality and feelings instead of playing something that someone else thinks is the way to do it.

### How do I get started?

Learn the very simple melody below. Make sure you can play it perfectly at a moderate walking tempo of about MM=72 to MM=80. Once you have done this, study the next few pages and we'll show you different ways of improvising around the melody.

Basic melody

Notice that
• The tune is rhythmically very simple, using only whole notes, half notes, and quarter notes.
• Symbols for the accompanying chords are placed above the melody. These can be played on any chordal instrument such as guitar or keyboard, or, listen to the tracks on the CD that accompanies this book. **All the notes in the melody belong to these accompanying chords.** The spelling of the basic chords is as follows: C=C E G; F=F A C; G7=G B D F.

Track No. 1 on the accompanying CD plays these chords so that you can hear the result of the first group of improvisations.

## What's a grace note?
A grace note is a very fast note inserted before the melody note.

## What does a grace note look like?
A grace note is a smaller sized note which usually takes the form of an 8th note with a diagonal line through the stem (♪).

## What notes can be used as grace notes?
From below, grace notes are usually a half-step below the melody note. For example if the melody note is E, the lower grace note would usually be a D♯, although D natural can also be used. From above, grace notes are usually a whole step or a half step above the melody note depending on the scale you're playing in. For example, in the scale of C you'd probably use the note A as an upper grace note to G. In the scale of F minor (which has four flats) you'd probably use an A♭. But these are only guidelines, not hard and fast rules.

## How do I play grace notes?
When the grace note is below the melody note it can be played three different ways:
• 1. Bow the grace note. Then, without releasing the pressure of your finger, slide up to the melody note. The letter S above a note means to slide.
• 2. Bow the grace note. Then, without releasing the pressure of your finger, hammer down with the next finger so that the melody note sounds without interrupting the bow. The letter H above a note means that note is played as a hammer-on.
• 3. Both the grace note and the melody note can be bowed. Always start with an up bow so that the melody note is played with a down bow.

Using the same finger to play grace notes

Using different fingers to play grace notes

Important: Because playing a grace note on a different string from the melody note is awkward or impossible, the A note in the 2nd measure must be played on the 3rd string, and the last two notes in the piece must be played on the 2nd string.

Important: The melody note is played on the beat. The time for the grace note is taken from the previous note.

## How do I play grace notes? (continued)

When the grace note is above the melody note it can be played in three different ways:
• 1. Finger the grace note with the same finger you will use for the melody note. Bow the grace note and—without releasing the pressure of the finger—slide down to the melody note. This works as long as the melody note is a fingered note, not an open string. The symbol S means to slide.

Example 7B.1  Sliding down from an upper grace note

• 2. Finger both the grace note and the melody note. Then pull the higher finger off the string with a sideways motion so that the melody note sounds clear without picking the string again. This technique is used with pizzicato and works well even if the melody note is an open string. The symbol P stands for this technique, called a pull-off.

Ex. 7B.2 Pulling-off from an upper grace note

• 3. Both the grace note and the melody note can be bowed Use a light up bow for the grace note so that the melody note is played with a down bow.

Ex. 7B.3 Bowing an upper grace note

As we mentioned previously, it's always good to use the next higher note in the scale as an upper grace note, but a note not in the scale can also be used depending on the effect you want. Generally grace notes that are not in the scale give you a more exotic and/or emotional effect than grace notes that are in the scale.

Ex. 7B.4 Upper grace notes that are not in the scale. Use slides, pull-offs, or bowing.

Two notes can also be used as grace notes. Play the following examples as hammer-ons, pull-offs, or bowing. Sliding is less effective because it tends to sound sloppy, but if you like the sound, use it!

Ex. 8.1  Double grace notes from below and above

Ex. 8.2  Double grace notes from both sides of the melody note. Again, use hammer-ons, pull-offs, or bowing, but not sliding.

Ex. 8.3 Various ways of playing triple grace notes. Use hammer-ons, pull-offs or bowing. If bowing, always start with an up bow so that you play the melody note with a down bow.

Ex. 8.4 Some examples of quadruple grace notes. These almost have to be bowed in order to get a clean sound. Start with an up bow so that the melody note gets a down bow.

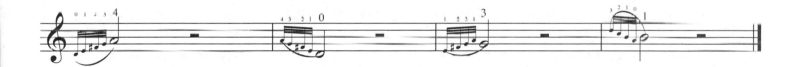

The next four sets of grace notes begin on the melody note. Then comes a higher note and finally the melody note. The first of these is called a **mordent** in classical music. Its symbol is ᙏ . All these embellishments should be played on a single string. When playing pizzicato, pluck the first note, then follow with a fast hammer-on followed by a pull-off. In other words, only pluck once for each measure. Or, use a continuous bow for all the notes.

These embellishments insert a lower tone between two melody notes. Play them like the mordents above. The first one is sometimes called an **inverted mordent** ( ᙏ ).

The symbol ∾ is called a **turn**. It means to play a series of four or five grace notes leading to the next note. Bow the whole figure. When playing pizz. you'll have to pluck each note unless you have unusually strong fingers.

can be played starting on the
note above the melody note

can be played starting on the melody note

5

Trills are a rapid alternation between the melody note and the note above. Up till about the time of J.S. Bach they usually began on the note above. Since then they usually begin on the melody note. One bow for the whole trill.

a short trill starting on
the melody note

a short trill starting on the note
above the melody note

a longer trill starting on the melody note

5

## What are neighbor notes?
Neighbor notes are notes that lie a half step or a whole step above or below a melody note.

## How are they notated?
They're written like any other note and are the same size as a normal note.

## How are neighbor notes used?
Neighbor notes are used to enhance melody notes. When the melody note is a chord tone it tends to sound a little bland, like scrambled eggs without salt. Adding a neighbor note gives the melody more interest and spice.

## Are they played fast, like grace notes?
No. Although they can be played almost as fast as a grace note, a better effect is to play them at least as long as an 8th note. They can be as long as the melody note or even longer. See examples below.

Using the same simple melody you learned on page 5, here are ways you can use upper neighbor notes (UN) and lower neighbor notes (LN) to enhance it.

Ex. 10B.1  Upper neighbors. All the other notes are chord tones.

Track 3

Ex. 10B.2  Lower neighbors that are in the scale

Ex. 10B.3  Lower neighbors that are a half step below the melody note

Here are four more variations mixing upper and lower neighbors. After completing this page, make up some original variations using the same techniques. You can use either the same four-bar melody, or pick a favorite tune and see what you can do with it.

This variation may sound a little strange to you. It uses many chromatic (not in the scale) neighbor notes.

This variation uses a steady stream of 8th notes, all of which are in the scale. It's typical of certain styles including Celtic and Bluegrass (which we'll see later in this book).

In this variation the neighbor notes are longer than the melody notes.

Still another variation that uses diatonic (in the scale) and chromatic (not in the scale) neighbor notes. Starting off the beat gives an exciting syncopated effect typical of some square dance tunes and ragtime.

## What is a passing tone?

A passing tone (PT) is a non-chord tone that connects two chord tones **by step**.

Ex.12B.1 The passing tones (PT) connect the chord tones by step.

## How does a passing tone differ from a neighbor note?

You can skip to a neighbor note from any chord tone. Passing tones are always approached by step.

Ex. 12B.2 Passing tones are approached by step. Neighbor notes can be approached by skip. (A skip is more than a whole step.)

## What is a diatonic passing tone?

The word diatonic simply means "in the scale." All the examples on this page are diatonic passing tones. Remember that the chord tones in a C chord are C E G; in an F chord, F A C; in a G7 chord, G B D F.

Ex. 12B.3 Diatonic passing tones and neighbor notes on the same melody. Notice the special fingering on the last nine notes which enables you to play the whole figure on one string.

Ex.12B.4 More neighbor notes and passing tones.

## What is a chromatic passing tone?

Chromatic passing tones connect chord tones by half steps. For example, if two chord tones are C and E, the chromatic passing tones between them would be C♯, D, and D♯.

As you can see, playing chromatic passing tones is more difficult than playing diatonic passing tones on the violin. Here's a new melody based on the same chords:

This variation uses diatonic passing tones.

Here chromatic passing tones are used.

Another variation that uses chromatic passing tones.

## What is a slide?

The slide is a very effective device for enhancing a melody. Because it's easy to do, many players overuse it so that it merely becomes an annoying mannerism. Like salt in your food, just because a little is a good thing doesn't mean that a lot is better.

## What kinds of slide are there?

Basically, there are three kinds of slide. To slide from one note to another, bow the first note and keep the pressure of the finger on the string as you slide to the second note. Be aware that the slide must begin with a fingered note and go to a higher (or lower) fingered note **on the same string**. The symbol for this type of slide is a diagonal line connecting the two notes with the letter "S" above it as in Example 14.1.

Ex. 14.1 Ascending and descending slides. Note the special fingerings so that each slide can be played on one string.

**Track 4**

Slides can also begin on an indefinite note and end on a fingered note. For this type of slide place the finger on the string, but lightly so that the string is muffled. Then bow the string, and as you slide toward the next note, gradually increase the pressure of your finger so that the melody note sounds clear. The symbol for this type of slide is a diagonal line leading up to the melody note with the letter "S" above it. See Ex. 14.2 below.

Ex. 14.2 Ascending slides starting with an indefinite note.

A third very effective type of slide begins on a fingered note and ends with an indefinite tone. To play it, bow the fingered note and as you slide away from it (up or down) gradually release the pressure of the finger. This effect is sometimes called a "fall" if it goes lower, and a "doit" (rhymes with "quoit") if it goes higher. The symbol for it is a curved line showing the direction of the fall or doit.

Descending slides starting with an indefinite note.

Ex.14.3 Doits

Falls

15

## What is a tremolo?
The tremolo is a rapid down- and up-bowing on a note or notes.

## Why is tremolo important?
Tremolo is another way of sustaining a tone on the violin. It's an effect that is often used to give a sense of anticipation or to create more tension than a tone sustained with a continuous bow.

## How will I know when to use tremolo?
Some meticulous composers and arrangers use three small hash marks through the stem of each note with the abbreviation "trem." above where tremolo is called for. See Ex. 15.1. But often it's a matter of taste. Certain styles such as Italian and Russian music use a lot of tremolo. Others such as jazz and country use it seldom. Since this is a book on improvisation, this is another opportunity for you to show your individuality and originality. Use tremolo when it sounds good to you.

## What can I do to make my tremolo sound smooth?
If you've never played tremolo, it will take a little work to train the muscles in your right wrist and forearm to produce a pleasing tone. Ex.15.2 is an exercise which will help you do this. If you're using a metronome (and we highly recommend it) start with MM=60 and make sure you can play the exercise smoothly, without hesitation, and with a pleasing tone. (If you don't have a metronome, MM=60 means one beat per second, a slow walking pace or one click on some clocks that mark seconds.) Then each time you play the exercise gradually increase the speed till you can play it at MM=120 or faster. (MM=120 is about march tempo.) The faster you play the tremolo, the smoother it will sound. Pay close attention to the bowing which—except for the quarter notes—should be down and up throughout.

Ex. 15.1 Plain melody notes

The same notes with tremolo. Play the tremolo using three different bowings: 1. at the point 2. middle of the bow 3. at the nut. Notice the differences in sound.

Ex. 15.2 Basic tremolo exercise. Keep the wrist relaxed. Play this exercise on various notes every day for a few minutes, gradually increasing the speed and we guarantee your tremolo will soon become smooth as silk.

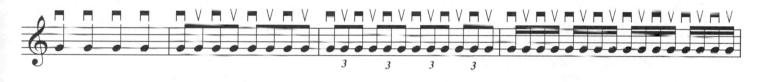

## IMPROVISING WITH MELODIES—SUMMING UP

So far in this book we have used the melody as the basis of all our variations. We have learned five different techniques for enhancing and varying a given melody:

### Grace notes:
Grace notes from a half step and a whole step below the melody note
Grace notes from a half step and a whole step above the melody note
Double grace notes from below and above
Triple and quadruple grace notes from above and below
Mordents, inverted mordents, turns and trills

### Neighbor notes:
Diatonic neighbor notes from below and above the melody note
Chromatic neighbor notes from below and above the melody note

### Passing tones:
Diatonic passing tones
Chromatic passing tones

### Slides:
Ascending and descending slides from melody note to melody note
Ascending and descending slides from an indefinite note to a melody note
Falls and doits

**Tremolo:** What it is, how to play it, and where to use it.

We suggest that you take a favorite tune and experiment with these techniques till you find variations that please you. Not every technique works on every tune. For example, most people would not consider a classical melody a suitable place to use slides. But who knows, you might be the person who figures out a new sound that combines classical melodies with techniques associated with rock and jazz (as did the group "Mannheim Steamroller" and the vocal group "Amici Forever.").

# A Bit of Music Theory

## What is a scale?
A scale is a series of tones that begins on the note that names the scale (called the root, tonic, or keynote) and ends on the same note an octave (eight notes) higher. For example, a C scale begins on the note C and continues up through D, E, F, G, A, B, and finally another C.

## What is an interval?
An interval is the space between two notes. To determine the name of an interval, just count on your fingers. The lower note is "1". Then count up the scale till you get to the note you want. For example, the interval between C and D is called a **second**. Between C and E the interval is a **third**. Between C and G is a **fifth**, and between C and the next higher C is eight notes called an **octave**.

## What is the interval of a half step?
A half step, also called a minor second, is the smallest interval used in traditional music. It is defined as the distance from one note to the next possible note, natural, sharp, or flat. For example, from C to D♭ is a half step. From D to E♭ is also a half step, and so on. Here's a complete list of all the possible half steps: C — D♭ or C♯— D—D♯ or E♭—E—F—F♯ or G♭—G—G♯ or A♭—A—A♯ or B♭—B—C.

## What is the interval of a whole step?
A whole step, also called a major second, equals two half steps. For example, from C to D is a whole step. From D to E is also a whole step. Here's a complete list of whole steps: C—D—E—F♯ or G♭—G♯ or A♭—A♯ or B♭—C. Starting with C♯ or D♭, the whole steps are: C♯ or D♭—D♯ or E♭—F—G—A—B—C♯ or D♭.

## Why do I need to know this?
Because scales are composed of a series of whole steps and half steps. So to understand scales, you should understand intervals.

## How many kinds of scales are there?
There are hundreds of scales, but don't panic! Only a few are used in most of the music you might hear. Most folk songs and bluegrass, all of country and western music and most jazz are written in either the major or minor scale. Examples of the most useful major and minor scales can be found on the following pages. Later in the book we'll also teach you some exotic scales used in Gypsy, Klezmer, Japanese, and Chinese musics.

## What is a chord?
A chord is a group of three or more tones that sound good together. It may be useful to think of the most common chords as being built in intervals of a third. For example, the C major chord can be thought of as the 1st, 3rd, and 5th notes of the C major scale, namely C E G. (Notice that from C to E is the interval of a third, and from E to G is also a third.) The F major chord can be thought of as the 4th, 6th, and 8th notes of the C major scale, namely F A C. Notice that these notes also are separated by thirds. The chord G7 (say "G seventh") can be thought of as the 5th, 7th, 2nd, and 4th notes of the C major scale, G B D F.

## What are the I, IV, and V7 chords?
In the key of C, because it begins on the first note of the scale, the C major chord is sometimes called the I chord (say "the one chord.") Similarly, because the F chord is built on the 4th step of the scale it's sometimes called the IV chord (the four chord.) Since G7 is built on the 5th step of the scale it's sometimes called the V7 (five-seven) chord.

## Why are these chords important?
The I, IV, and V7 chords are the most important chords in any major or minor key. Guitar players know that hundreds of songs can be accompanied using only these three chords.

### What is a major scale?

A major scale consists of eight notes: The root or keynote which is followed by an ascending series of whole steps and half steps until the higher keynote is reached. For example, the C major scale consists of the notes C D E F G A B C.

### In what order are the whole steps and half steps?

In a major scale (and only in a major scale!) the intervals occur in this order: whole step, whole step, half step, whole step, whole step, whole step, half step. If you've done it right you should now be at the keynote again.

### Can you give me a "for instance"?

From C to D is a whole step; from D to E is a whole step; from E to F is a half step; from F to G, G to A, and A to B are all whole steps; from B up to C is a half step. An easy way to remember this is "2 and a half, 3 and a half."

What follows are the most useful major scales with the whole steps and half steps clearly marked.

The C major scale

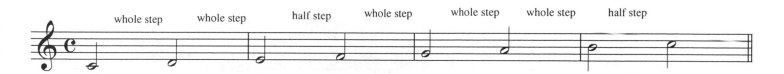

The G major scale. In order to make the scale conform to the pattern of whole steps and half steps, the note F must be raised a half step to F♯.

The D major scale. In order to make this scale conform to the pattern of whole steps and half steps, both the F and the C must be raised a half step to F♯ and C♯.

The A major scale. To make this scale conform to the pattern of whole steps and half steps the F, C, and G all have to be raised a half step to F♯, C♯, and G♯.

The E major scale. To make this scale conform to the pattern of whole steps and half steps, the F, C, G, and D all have to be raised to F♯, C♯, G♯, and D♯.

The B major scale. Five notes must be sharped: F, C, G, D, and A.

**The F major scale** To make this scale conform to the major scale pattern of whole steps and half steps, the B must be lowered a half step to B♭.

**The B♭ major scale** To make this scale conform, both the B's and the E must be lowered a half step to B♭ and E♭.

**The E♭ major scale** B, E, and A must be lowered a half step to make this scale conform to the major scale pattern of whole steps and half steps.

**The A♭ major scale.** B, E, A, and D must be lowered a half step to B♭, E♭, A♭, and D♭ to make this scale conform to the major scale pattern of whole steps and half steps.

Although these aren't all the major scales, they are the most useful. You probably won't need to play any of the others (F♯(six sharps)C♯(seven sharps)D♭(five flats)G♭(six flats) C♭(seven flats)).

An important reminder: If you're only going to read music, that is, play things that other people have written, knowing your scales and chords is somewhat less important. But since this is a book that deals with improvising, knowledge of scales and chords is crucial!

## How can I use major scales to improvise?

You can use major scales to improvise in two ways:

1. If you're still using the melody as your basis, you can use scales to fill the spaces between the melody notes. Just make sure the scale you're using is the same one the piece is written in. Ex. 20.1 is a basic melody in the key of G. It has large skips in it, so Ex. 20.2 demonstrates how you can use the G major scale (G A B C D E F# G) to fill in the gaps between the melody notes. The accompanying chords in the key of G are the I, IV, and V7 chords: G (G B D), C (C E G), and D7 (D F# A C).

Ex. 20.1  Basic melody in the key of G

Ex. 20.2  Using the G major scale to fill the spaces between melody notes

2. Another way to improvise is to ignore the melody and run the scale. This technique is often used after the melody has been established. For example, on the first chorus play the melody with a few variations. Second chorus, play the melody again, but with added passing tones and neighbor notes. Third (and other choruses), play variations based on the scale, but not suggesting the melody. Last chorus, play the melody again with or without an added final section called by its Italian name, "coda".

Example 20.3 uses as its basis the same G major melody, but ignores the actual melody notes and uses the G major scale to develop variations.

Ex. 20.3 Ignoring the melody notes and running the G major scale

Here is an improvisation on a familiar tune in the key of G. This variation uses the G major scale, as well as other techniques you have learned such as neighbor notes, passing tones, etc. The accompanying chords are the I, IV, and V7 chords  G, C, D7 plus one other chord, A7, which is spelled A C# E G.

JINGLE BELLS (variations suggest the melody)

This variation ignores the melody and runs the G scale.

Now it's your turn. Use the rhythm track on the CD to play your own variations.

## What are minor scales?

When you hear the word "minor" in music you should always think "lowered third." For example, the third note of the G *major* scale is B; the third note of the G *minor* scale is B♭. The third note of the D *major* scale is F♯; the third note of the D *minor* scale is F natural.

## Does this apply to chords also?

Yes. The third of a C *major* chord is E; the third of a C *minor* chord is E♭. The third of an A7 chord is C♯; the third of an A *minor* 7th chord is C natural.

## How many kinds of minor scale are there?

There are three kinds of minor scale in common use: the **natural minor**, the **harmonic minor**, and the **melodic minor**.

## How do you determine the key signature of a minor scale?

Minor scales borrow their key signatures from the major scale which is three half steps higher. For example, the G minor scale has the same key signature (two flats) as the B♭ major scale. The E minor scale has the same key signature as G major, one sharp. Because they share the same key signature, E minor is called the relative minor of G major; conversely, G major is the relative major of E minor.

## What is a natural minor scale?

Since the B♭ major scale uses a key signature of two flats, B♭ and E♭, the G minor scale uses the same key signature but starts and ends on G. The notes in a G natural minor scale are G A B♭ C D E♭ F G. We'll discuss the natural minor in greater detail in the section on modes.

## What is a harmonic minor scale?

The harmonic minor is the same as the natural minor except that **the 7th note of the scale is raised a half step**. In the G minor scale the 7th note is F, so the G harmonic minor scale uses an F♯ instead of an F. The notes in a G harmonic minor scale are G A B♭ C D E♭ F♯ G. The B♭ and E♭ are usually in the key signature, but the F♯ is written in every time it appears.

## Why is it called "harmonic"?

Because the chords used are derived from this scale. The most important chords in each harmonic minor scale are the I, IV, and V7 chords, just like in the major scale. But in a minor scale both the I and IV chords are minor instead of major; the V7 is an ordinary seventh chord, the same as in major. For example, the I chord in the key of G minor is a G minor chord (G B♭ D); The IV chord is a C minor chord (C E♭ G). The V7 chord is a D7 chord (D F♯ A C).

On the next page are eight of the most useful harmonic minor scales on the violin with the half steps, whole steps, and in one case one-and-a-half steps marked.

The **F harmonic minor scale** has the same key signature as A♭ major, so B, E, A, and D are flatted. Then the E is changed to a natural when it appears in the music.

The **C harmonic minor scale** has the same signature as E♭ major. so B, E, and A are flatted. Then the B is changed to a natural when it appears in the music.

The **G harmonic minor scale**. Has the same key signature as B♭ major, so B and E are played as B♭ and E♭.

The **D harmonic minor scale** has the same key signature as F major, so the B is played as B♭.

The **A harmonic minor scale** has the same key signature as C major, and uses no sharps or flats.

The **E harmonic minor scale** has the same key signature as G major, so the F's are played as F♯'s.

The **B harmonic minor scale** has the same key signature as D major, so F and C are sharped.

The **F♯ harmonic minor scale** has the same key signature as A major, so F, C, and G are sharped.

## Improvising with harmonic minor scales

Any of the techniques you've learned so far can be used in minor as well as major. Here is a short example, first the basic melody in D minor, then a series of four-bar variations that use many of the techniques you've learned so far.

1st variation sticks fairly close to the melody.

2nd variation uses upper and lower neighbor notes to the basic melody.

3rd variation ignores melody and just runs the scale.

4th variation uses slides and trills.

5th variation restates the melody, but using tremolo.

## Melodic minor scales

As the name suggests, melodic minor scales are most often used for constructing melodies. Melodic minor scales have two forms: ascending, they're just like a major scale with a lowered third. So the G melodic minor ascends with the notes G A B♭ C D E F♯ G. The descending form is just like the natural minor so that the descending form of the G melodic minor has the notes G F E♭ D C B♭ A G. Here are six of the most useful melodic minor scales:

C melodic minor scale

G melodic minor scale

D melodic minor scale

A melodic minor scale

E melodic rninor scale

B melodic minor scale

## Improvising with the Melodic Minor Scale

Below is a melody in A minor, followed by five four-bar variations that make use of many of the techniques you have learned. When using the melodic minor, the IV chord is sometimes minor (Dm) and sometimes major (D).

MINOR MOOD (basic melody)

1st variation sticks fairly close to the melody.

2nd variation uses diatonic and chromatic neighbor notes and passing tones.

3rd variation ignores the melody notes and runs the scale.

4th variation reverts to quarter notes, using diatonic passing tones and neighbor notes.

Final variation restates the melody an octave lower with tremolo.

## Improvising with Modes

### What are modes?
Modes are a series of notes separated by whole steps and half steps. Like scales, they begin and end on notes an octave apart.

### How do modes differ from scales?
Sometimes modes are the same as certain scales. Other modes have the half steps and whole steps in varying places.

### When were modes invented?
Their origins are lost in history, but they probably were in use 2500 or more years ago.

### When did they fall out of use?
Modes were the common form of musical expression until about the 16th century when they were gradually replaced by major and minor scales. Virtually all classical music, popular, and folk songs composed between 1650 and 1900 was written in major or minor scales.

### Why study them now?
About a hundred years ago modes were rediscovered, and because they had a different sound from major and minor scales, they sounded fresh and unusual. Many rock tunes are written in modes (e.g. The Beatles' "Paperback Writer") and it is possible to find old folk songs that apparently date from the days that modes were in common use (e.g. "Scarborough Fair").

### How many modes are there?
There are seven modes, six of which are still in use. Modes are named after places in ancient Greece.

### What are the seven modes and what notes does each one contain?
Originally the modes used only the natural notes (notes without sharps or flats). Or, you can think of them as consisting of the white keys on the piano.
The **Ionian** (Eye-o-nee-an) **mode** is identical to the C major scale: C D E F G A B C
The **Dorian** (Dor-ee-an) **mode** uses the notes D E F G A B C D
The **Phrygian** (Fridj-ee-an) **mode** uses the notes E F G A B C D E
The **Lydian** (Lid-ee-an) **mode** uses the notes F G A B C D E F
The **Mixolydian** (Mix-o-lid-ee-an) **mode** uses the notes G A B C D E F G
The **Aeolian** (Ay-oh-lee-an) **mode** is the same as the A natural minor scale: A B C D E F G A
The **Locrian** (Low-cree-an) **mode** (rarely if ever used) uses the notes B C D E F G A B

On the next few pages we describe each mode in detail and give examples of improvisations based on them.

## The Ionian mode

The Ionian mode is the same as the C major scale: C D E F G A B C. The most important chords in this mode are the I chord C (C E G), the IV chord F (F A C), and the V7 chord G7 (G B D F). Here is an improvisation in the Ionian mode. After you learn it, try your own improvisation against the rhythm track.

IONIAN ITEM

## The Dorian mode

On the keyboard, the Dorian mode consists of the white keys between D and D an octave higher: D E F G A B C D. This sea chantey is in the Dorian mode. The I chord in the Dorian mode is D minor (D F A). Other important chords are the VII chord C (C E G) the III chord F (F A C) and the IV chord G (G B D).

THE DRUNKEN SAILOR (basic melody)

THE DRUNKEN SAILOR (variation)

After you learn this tune and variation, develop your own improvisation using the Dorian mode.

## The Phrygian mode

This mode is closely associated with Spanish music, especially Flamenco. It consists of the notes E F G A B C D E. The most important chords in the Phrygian mode are the IV chord A minor (ACE), the III chord G (G B D), the II chord F (F A C) and the I chord which is almost always played as E major (E G# B) although technically the note G# is not in the mode. Here is a typical four-bar sequence and several variations on it.

THE SPANISH TINGE (basic melody)

1st variation sticks close to the melody

2nd variation is more free using passing tones and neighbor notes

3rd variation ignores melody and just runs the mode freely

4th variation introduces a triplet figure on repeated chord tones

5th variation spells out each chord (with one passing tone)

Final variation goes into the upper register

After you learn this melody and variations, try your hand at making up your own. This is particularly effective if you can find a guitarist to play chords for you. Or, use the rhythm track.

## The Lydian mode

The Lydian mode is like an F major scale but with a B natural instead of a B♭. The B natural gives it a piquant sound that some jazz players like. It is also characteristic of some Hungarian folk music and shows up in the music of Bela Bartok. The notes in the Lydian mode are F G A B C D E F. The main chords are the I chord F (F A C), the II chord G (G B D) and the V chord C (C E G).

LYDIA'S LUNCH (Basic melody)

The first variation uses a more or less steady stream of 8th notes all from the Lydian mode.

The second variation ignores the melody and creates rhythmic figures based on chord tones.

Our final variation is kind of tricky to play because it uses many chromatic notes. But the effect is worth it!

## The Mixolydian mode

This mode is like a G major scale but using an F natural instead of F$\sharp$. The notes are G A B C D E F G. To illustrate this mode we have chosen "Old Joe Clark, a famous square dance tune which is in the Mixolydian mode. The most important chords are the I chord G (G B D) and the VII chord F (F A C).

OLD JOE CLARK (basic melody)

Our first variation uses double bowing to add motion and excitement.

Note the use of diatonic lower neighbor notes in this variation.

Our final variation uses chromatic lower neighbor notes to add a little spice.

## The Aeolian mode

This ancient mode tends to have a sweet, sad sound, as in the famous Civil War song "When Johnny Comes Marching Home" (which probably was based on a Celtic melody). We've chosen an old folk song to illustrate the Aeolian mode. The notes are A B C D E F G A. The main chords are the I chord A minor (A C E), the VII chord G (G B D), the III chord C (C E G) the VI chord F (F A C), and the V chord E minor or major (E G B or E G♯ B).

SHADY GROVE (basic melody)

The first variation makes use of the fact that the A can be played open or stopped.

The second variation makes use of legato bowing. See how smoothly you can play it.

The final variation is very simple. However, it is an opportunity to show off how expressively you can play.

Now you try it.

36

## The Locrian mode

This mode consists of the notes B C D E F G A B. Because the dissonant interval B–F (called the "devil in music" by early musicians) is so prominent, ancient musicians found the mode unusable unless the F was sharped or the B was flatted. If the F is sharped, the mode sounds exactly like a Phrygian mode starting on B. If the B is flatted, it sounds like a Lydian mode starting on B♭. However, it is interesting to note that the accidentals F♯ and B♭ are still the most commonly used. F♯ is the first sharp in a key signature that uses sharps. B♭ is the first flat in a key signature that uses flats. But since the Locrian mode is so rare or duplicates other modes, there's no need to concern ourselves with it here.

## Can modes be transposed to other notes?

In ancient usage the modes were always played on the notes we have described. But nowadays a mode can start on any note as long as the half steps and whole steps remain in the same relative places.

## Can you give me an example?

The Dorian mode consists of the notes D E F G A B C D. All the steps in this mode are whole steps except for E–F and B-C which are half steps. Since these occur between the 2nd to 3rd steps and between the 6th to 7th steps, when you start the mode on a different note, sharps or flats must be added so that the half steps still fall between the 2nd and 3rd steps and between the 6th and 7th steps. We don't have room to illustrate every possibility, but the examples below will suggest how to go about transposing modes to other notes.

## The six most important modes, what notes they contain, where the half steps lie, and which are the most important chords (key chord in bold face type)

The Ionian mode:  C D E F G A B C half steps between the 3rd and 4th steps and the 7th and 8th steps; most important chords **C** F G

The Dorian mode:  D E F G A B C D  half steps between the 2nd and 3rd steps and the 6th and 7th steps; most important chords **Dm** G C F

The Phrygian mode: E F G A B C D E half steps between the 1st and 2nd steps and the 5th and 6th steps; most important chords Am G F **E major or minor**

The Lydian mode: F G A B C D E F  half steps between the 4th and 5th and the 7th and 8th steps; most important chords **F** G C

The Mixolydian mode: G A B C D E F  half steps between the 3rd and 4th and the 6th and 7th steps **G** F C

The Aeolian mode: A B C D E F G A half steps between the 2nd and 3rd steps and the 5th and 6th steps; most important chords **Am** G Dm C

Here are a few examples:

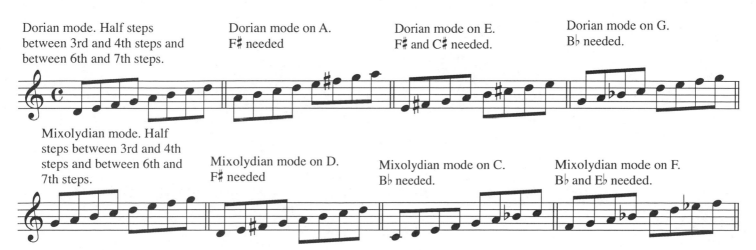

Dorian mode. Half steps between 3rd and 4th steps and between 6th and 7th steps.

Dorian mode on A. F♯ needed

Dorian mode on E. F♯ and C♯ needed.

Dorian mode on G. B♭ needed.

Mixolydian mode. Half steps between 3rd and 4th steps and between 6th and 7th steps.

Mixolydian mode on D. F♯ needed

Mixolydian mode on C. B♭ needed.

Mixolydian mode on F. B♭ and E♭ needed.

## Improvising with specialty scales

So far, all the scales and modes we've studied have one thing in common: they contain seven different notes. But many tunes—especially folk songs—use other scales with fewer notes. For example, the American murder ballad "Pretty Polly" is based on a six-note scale sometimes called a hexachord. This scale contains the notes D E F G A and C. That is, it's just like the Dorian mode, but with the 6th step (B) missing. When you improvise on this tune you may find it most effective if you use only notes found in this hexachord.

Track 7

PRETTY POLLY

American folk song

I used to be a rambler and I strayed from town to town,
I used to be a rambler and I strayed from town to town,
I courted Pretty Polly and her beauty's never been found.

I courted Pretty Polly the livelong night,
I courted Pretty Polly the livelong night,
Then left her the next morning before it was light.

## What is a pentatonic scale?

As its name implies, the pentatonic scale contains only five notes. For example, the C pentatonic scale consists of the notes C D E G and A. That is, it's just like the C major scale with the 4th and 7th steps omitted.

## Why is this scale very important?

Pentatonic scales are used in the music of many peoples around the world especially in Chinese, American Indian, South American, and African music. But most importantly for American fiddle players, it is an important resource for improvising, especially in Bluegrass style. This is because when you use, say, an F pentatonic scale against an F chord, *any* note you play will sound good. It's impossible to make a mistake! For example, the first section of "Oh Susanna" is based on the F pentatonic scale; it uses only the notes F G A C and D. The variation that follows also uses the same notes, but in different combinations.

OH SUSANNA (basic melody, 1st section)

The first variation uses the F pentatonic scale, F G A C D.

Another variation using the F pentatonic scale

The next folk song is based on the C pentatonic scale: C D E G A.

SHORTNIN' BREAD

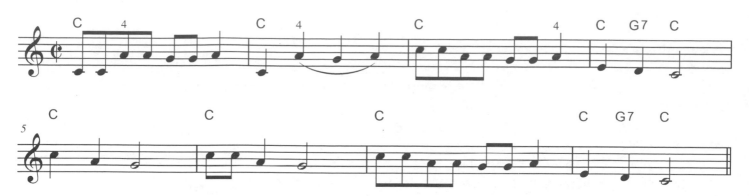

1st variation uses only notes in the C pentatonic scale

2nd variation uses notes of the C pentatonic scale but expands into the upper register.
Follow the fingering carefully for best results.

3rd variation adds grace notes and chromatic (not in the scale) neighbor notes.

Incredible as it might seem, some songs use only four notes, yet can have a terrific emotional impact. This Appalachian ballad uses only the notes A C D and E (called a tetrachord), yet the legendary folksinger, Leadbelly, and Kurt Cobain of Nirvana both recorded very powerful versions.

IN THE PINES (basic melody)

The first variation uses the same notes but in a different order

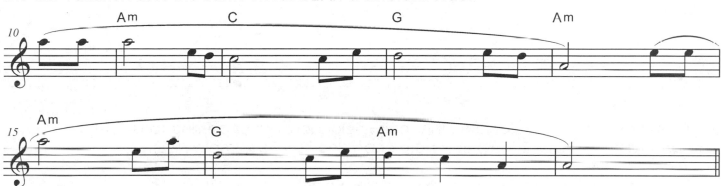

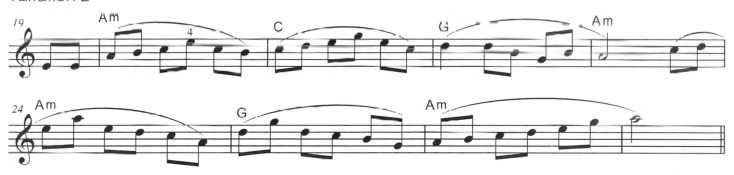

Although it is possible to improvise using only four notes, it is rather limiting. In this variation we have added B and G to the tetrachord A C D E to form an A minor hexachord, A B C D E G A.

Variation 2

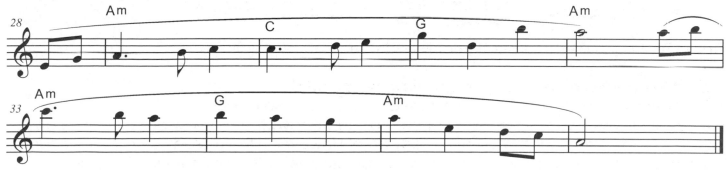

The final variation introduces a new rhythm and gives you a chance to show how expressively you can play.

Now you try it. Use the rhythm track on the CD.

# Improvising by adding notes to the melody

## What is a double stop?
Playing two notes at the same time.

## Why use double stops?
Double stops make a melody sound richer and fuller. They are used in every type of music from classical to Bluegrass.

## How do I know which added notes will sound good?
To answer this question we'll need to go into a little music theory. The general rules are these: If the melody note is a chord tone, the added note should be a chord tone.

Ex. 39.1
In this example the melody is always a chord tone. The added note below the melody is also a chord tone. Remember the spelling of the basic chords in the key of C: C=C E G; F=F A C; G7=G B D F.

If the melody note is a diatonic (in the scale) neighbor note or passing tone, the added note should be a diatonic neighbor note or passing tone. (Example 39.2)

Ex. 39.2  The same melody with added diatonic neighbor notes (N) and passing tones (PT).

If the melody note is a chromatic (not in the scale) neighbor note or passing tone, the added note should be a chromatic neighbor note or passing tone. (Example 39.3)

Ex. 39.3
The same melody with added chromatic neighbor notes (N) and passing tones (PT).

(These examples are for illustration only and need not be practiced.)

## Should the added note be above or below the melody?
The ear tends to pick out the higher note as the melody, so adding a note below the melody is always good. A note can also be added above the melody, but you need good bow control to bring out the lower melody note. However, if the melody is well-known, or if the higher note always stays the same, you can assume that your listeners will be able to pick out the melody without difficulty.

You'll find some practical examples of these techniques on the next two pages.

Here's a country style tune that's arranged in double stops. The melody is always the higher note. Especially notice the use of diatonic and chromatic passing tones in both the melody and harmony.

JUST LOPIN' ALONG

Track 8

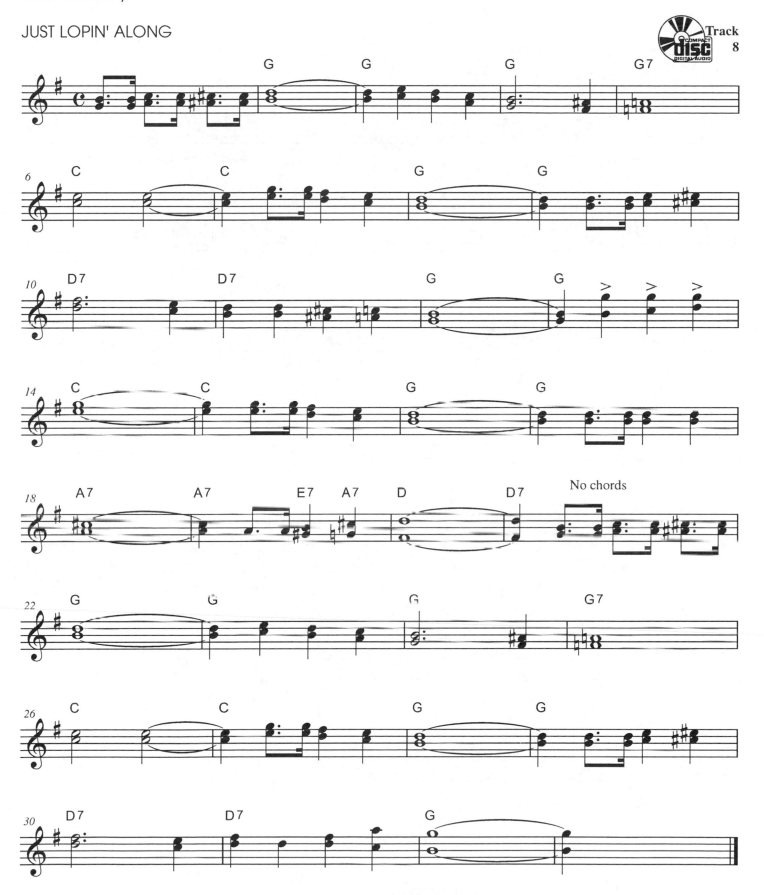

This waltz, which is the Missouri state song, is arranged using double stops with the melody sometimes above and sometimes below the harmony note. Pay special attention to the use of chromatic neighbor notes in both the melody and harmony. For a better effect, play the 8th notes long short, long short, instead of even.

THE MISSOURI WALTZ

John Eppel

44

## Using an open string as a drone

A very nice effect is to use an open string as a drone or pedal point. The open string is played with each melody note. The melody note is played on the string below it regardless of whether the drone fits with the chord. In this arrangement the drone is the open A string; the melody is always below it on the D string. In the first measure the A note is played on the 2nd string open and also on the 3rd string.

BLACK-EYED SUSIE

Track 9

All I want in this creation's
A pretty little wife and a big plantation
Chorus:
Hey, little black-eyed Susie,
Hey, little black-eyed Susie,
Hey, little black-eyed Susie, hey!

Love my wife, I love my baby,
Love my biscuits sopped in gravy
Chorus:
Hey, little black-eyed Susie,
Hey, little black-eyed Susie,
Hey, little black-eyed Susie, hey!

## Improvising with Chords

### What is a chord?
A chord is a group of three or more different notes that sound good together. For example, the C major chord consists of the notes C, E, and G. The D minor chord contains the notes D, F, and A. The G7 chord contains the notes G, B, D, and F. These notes can occur in any order; the C chord can be spelled C E G, E G C, G C E, E C G and so on. Notes can also be doubled: The C chord can have two C's, two E's, and/or two G's.

### What kinds of chords are there?
There are dozens of different types of chords, but on the violin the overwhelming majority of the ones you'll need are either major, minor, or 7th chords.

### How are chords spelled?
Chords are generally built in intervals of a third. For example, the C chord (when not specified, we're always talking about a major chord) consists of the notes C E G. From C to E is a major third (two whole steps or four half steps); from E to G is a minor third (a whole step and a half step or three half steps). On the other hand, the D minor chord which has the notes D F A has a minor third between D and F, and a major third between F and A. The G7 chord takes a G major chord (G B D) and adds another minor third above it (F).

Here is a chart that tells you how to spell every possible major, minor, and seventh chord. The more important ones are in bold face type.

| Root tone | Major chord | Minor chord | Seventh chord |
|---|---|---|---|
| **C** | **C E G** | **C E♭ G** | **C E G B♭** |
| C♯ | C♯ E♯ G♯ | C♯ E G♯ | C♯ E♯ G♯ B |
| D♭ | D♭ F A♭ | D♭ F♭ A♭ | D♭ F A♭ C♭ |
| **D** | **D F♯ A** | **D F A** | **D F♯ A C** |
| E♭ | E♭ G B♭ | E♭ G♭ B♭ | E♭ G B♭ D♭ |
| **E** | **E G♯ B** | **E G B** | **E G♯ B D** |
| **F** | **F A C** | **F A♭ C** | **F A C E♭** |
| F♯ | F♯ A♯ C♯ | F♯ A C♯ | F♯ A♯ C♯ E |
| G♭ | G♭ B♭ D♭ | G♭ B♭♭(A) D♭ | G♭ B♭ D♭ F♭ |
| **G** | **G B D** | **G B♭ D** | **G B D F** |
| A♭ | A♭ C E♭ | A♭ C♭ E♭ | A♭ C E♭ G♭ |
| **A** | **A C♯ E** | **A C E** | **A C♯ E G** |
| B♭ | B♭ D F | B♭ D♭ F | B♭ D F A♭ |
| **B** | **B D♯ F♯** | **B D F♯** | **B D♯ F♯ A** |
| C♭ | C♭ E♭ G♭ | C♭ E♭♭(D) G♭ | C♭ E♭ G♭ B♭♭(A) |

## Common major chords in various inversions

The word "inversion" means the rearranging of the notes of a chord in a different order. If the root of the chord (the note that names the chord) is the lowest note, the chord is in root position. If the third of the chord is the lowest note the chord is in 1st inversion. If the fifth of the chord is the lowest note the chord is in 2nd inversion.

(These examples are for reference only and need not be played)

C (contains the notes C E G)

D (contains the notes D F♯ A)

E (contains the notes E G♯ B)

F (contains the notes F A C)

G (contains the notes G B D)

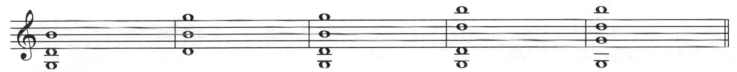

A (contains the notes A C♯ E)

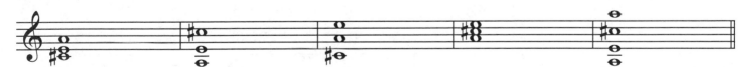

B♭ (contains the notes B♭ D F)

B (contains the notes B D♯ F♯)

## Common minor chords in various inversions

The abbreviation for a minor chord is a small "m" or "min". Remember that any note in a chord may be doubled. A note (especially the fifth of the chord) may be omitted. Here are some practical examples of the most common minor chords.

Cm (contains the notes C E♭ G)

C#m (contains the notes C# E G#)

Dm (contains the notes D F A)

Em (contains the notes E G B)

Fm (contains the notes  F A♭ C)

F#m (contains the notes F# A C#)

Gm (contains the notes G B♭ D)

Am (contains the notes A C E)

Bm (contains the notes B D F#)

## Common seventh chords in various inversions

Because seventh chords contain four different notes, it's almost always better to omit one note, usually the fifth or the root. The abbreviation for a seventh chord is the numeral "7". If the seventh is the lowest note, the chord is in 3rd inversion.

C7 (contains the notes C E G B♭)

D7 (contains the notes D F♯ A C)

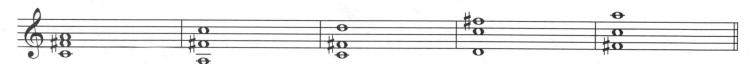

E7 (contains the notes E G♯ B D)

F7 (contains the notes F A C E♭)

F♯7 (contains the notes F♯ A♯ C♯ E)

G7 (contains the notes G B D F)

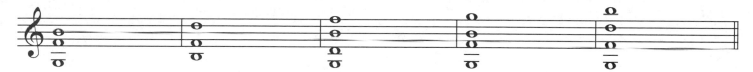

A7 (contains the notes A C♯ E G)

B7 (contains the notes B D♯ F♯ A)

## How can I create Improvisations using chords?

Chords can be used to create accompaniments for singers and soloists. Here's a sample chord progression with six variations. If you can keep your fingers down on the entire chord you'll get a smoother result... especially when playing pizzicato.

The Italian word "arpeggio" (ar-PED-joe) literally means "like a harp. "It means to break up chords into individual notes. Here's a simple arpeggio pattern in 4/4. It sounds best when played fast. It also works very well when played pizzicato.

ARPEGGIO PATTERN No. 1

ARPEGGIO PATTERN No. 2 A similar pattern, but using 8th notes. This works better at slower tempos.

ARPEGGIO PATTERN No. 3 A similar pattern adapted to 3/4 time. Choose your own bowing or pizz.

ARPEGGIO PATTERN No. 4 There's no need to use every note in every chord. The next pattern uses notes only on the A, D, and G strings, yet sounds complete and satisfying.

ARPEGGIO PATTERN No. 5 A similar pattern in 3/4 time.

ARPEGGIO PATTERN No. 6 A similar pattern in 4/4, but on the E, A, and D strings.

Now make up your own patterns. Then adapt them to other chords.

## Using neighbor notes with arpeggios

Sometimes very nice effects can be obtained by substituting a neighbor note for a chord tone in an arpeggio pattern.

ARPEGGIO PATTERN No. 7 This is a variation on Arpeggio Pattern No. 2. A neighbor note takes the place of a chord tone in the first half of the measure. Then the chord tone is sounded in the second half. Upper neighbor notes are marked UN.

ARPEGGIO PATTERN No. 8 In this variation a lower neighbor note (LN) takes the place of a chord tone in the first half of each measure.

ARPEGGIO PATTERN No. 9 Although all the neighbor notes we've shown you are played on the E string, it also sounds good to use them on lower strings. Here's a variation on Arpeggio Pattern No. 5.

ARPEGGIO PATTERN No. 10 A similar pattern to No. 6, but making use of upper and lower neighbor notes (UN and LN).

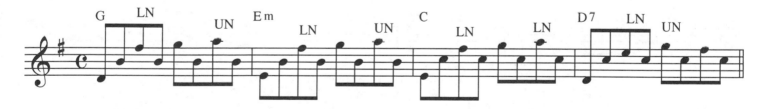

ARPEGGIO PATTERN No. 11 This pattern combines double stops with arpeggios.

# Part 2 – Tunes and Styles

Country and Western music is based on folk styles of years past, especially sentimental ballads and fast hoedowns from the 19th century and even earlier. The next song began as a sailor's lament called "O, Bury Me Not in the Deep, Deep Sea" written in about 1850. The cowboy words are anonymous.

Track 10

BURY ME NOT ON THE LONE PRAIRIE (basic melody)                    Music by George N. Allen

Now try your hand at it. If you stick to the G pentatonic scale anything you play will sound good!

# Country and Western Styles (cont.)

This old hobo song is ideal for building improvisations. The basic melody is a simple 12-bar tune which uses one new chord, E7. The notes in E7 are E G♯ B and D.

RAILROAD BILL (basic melody)

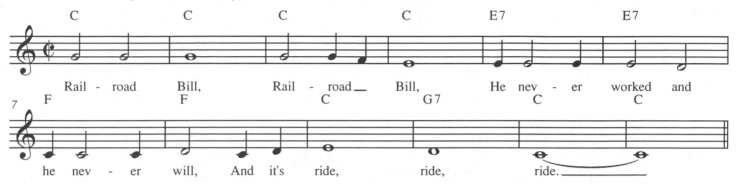

Variation 1 The melody is played an octave higher. This puts it into a brighter, more penetrating register. Then a harmony note is added below the melody.

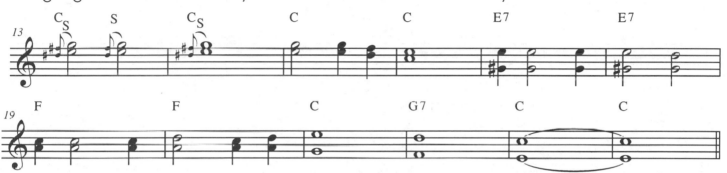

Variation 2 The melody still can be found, and the steady stream of 8th notes adds a lot of excitement.

Variation 3 uses syncopation (accented off-beats) and departs almost entirely from the basic melody.

# Country Waltz

Waltzes are a very popular country style in 3/4 time. All the techniques for improvising work, but now use only three beats in each measure. This cowboy classic has a simple but poignant melody.

BEAUTIFUL BROWN EYES

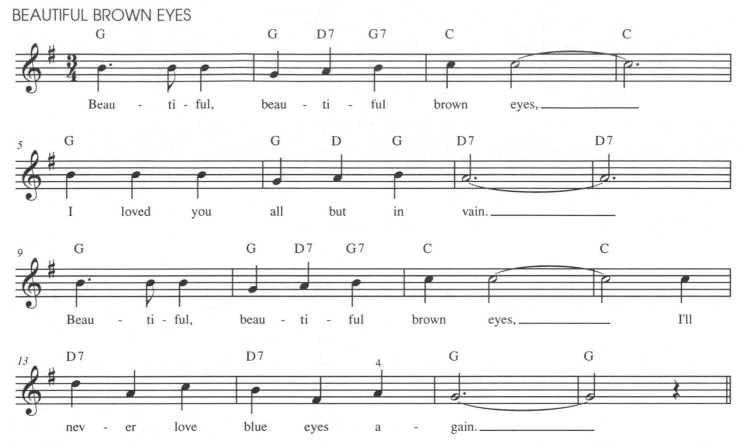

Beau - ti - ful, beau - ti - ful brown eyes,_____ I loved you all but in vain._____ Beau - ti - ful, beau - ti - ful brown eyes,_____ I'll nev - er love blue eyes a - gain._____

Variation 1 adds harmony notes above the melody, and occasional runs of 8th notes to fill in the dead spots.

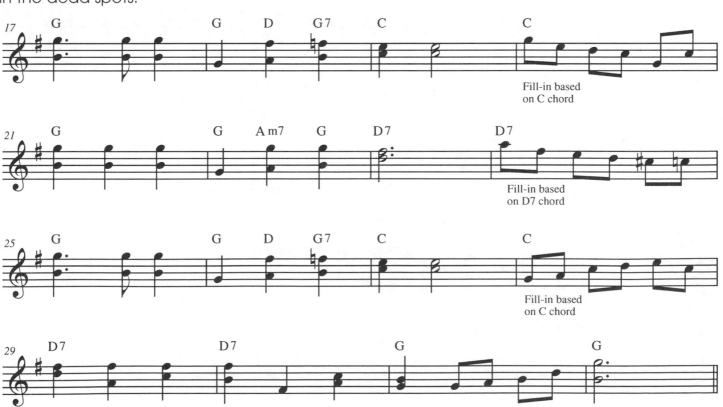

Fill-in based on C chord

Fill-in based on D7 chord

Fill-in based on C chord

The next variation adds harmony notes below the melody. Where you see a bracket sign see if you can make up a fill-in of your own.

BEAUTIFUL BROWN EYES (Variation 2)

The final variation keeps a stream of 8th notes going. Yet, the melody is still recognizable.

# Bluegrass Fiddle

Bluegrass music developed in the late 1920s as an outgrowth of other country styles including the famous Carter Family recordings and especially the Bill Monroe band. The fiddle, along with mandolin, guitar, and five-string banjo, gave Bluegrass its characteristic sound. Many Bluegrass standards originally were fiddle tunes mostly by anonymous writers. Here's a traditional fiddle tune, "The Eighth of January," which singer-songwriter Jimmy Driftwood used for his famous hit song "The Battle of New Orleans." (January 8, 1815 was the date of General Andrew Jackson's great victory over the British near New Orleans.) Use alternating down and up bows and follow the fingering carefully.

THE EIGHTH OF JANUARY (basic melody)

Track 11

For our first variation we have limited this solo to the same notes, but have sequenced them differently. When you have created a new solo and are uncertain whether it works with the chords of the original tune, have a friend play the chords while you lay down the solo. Or, tape the chords and play the solo over them.

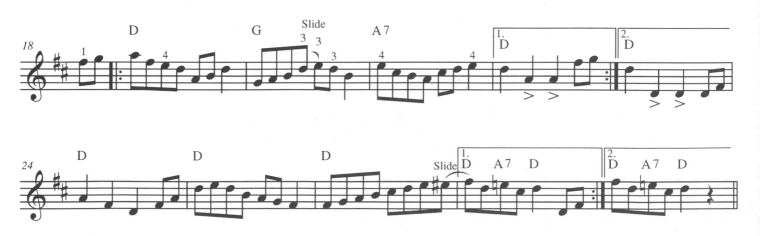

## HAMMERING ON

The third variation of "The Eighth of January" makes use of a left hand technique called "hammering on", used in combination with pizzicato. In this technique the left hand plays a note without any plucking from the right hand. For example, the fourth note of the solo is a hammered note. Play the open D string, then hammer the 1st finger down on the E note without plucking again. Try it slowly. You should hear two notes, the D followed by the E. Hammered notes are marked with an H.

THE EIGHTH OF JANUARY (3rd variation)

The next variation moves up to the 3rd position. *
First learn the 3rd position D major scale, then try the final variation below.

THE EIGHTH OF JANUARY (4th variation)

* Throughout this book positions are named like guitarists and mandolin players name them.

# Bluegrass (cont.)

"Little Maggie" is an old-time country tune that works well in Bluegrass style. The basic melody is a simple one in the Mixolydian mode (see p. 35). The accompaniment uses only two chords; this tests the limits of your creativity.

LITTLE MAGGIE (basic melody)

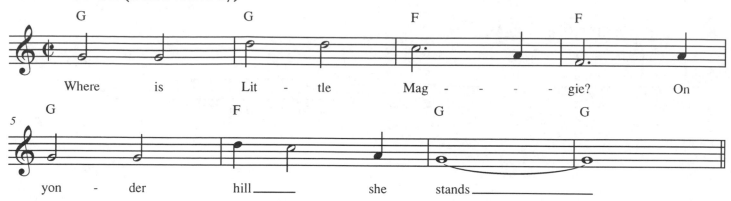

Variation 1 uses similar notes to those in the melody, played pizzicato (plucked) and staying within the Mixolydian mode.

Sometimes—especially at fast tempos like this one—it sounds great to pick notes out of the chords and play them rhythmically. The notes in the G chord are G B D; in the F chord, F A C.
Variation 2

Variation 3 continues in a similar vein, but moves around more with a touch of syncopation.

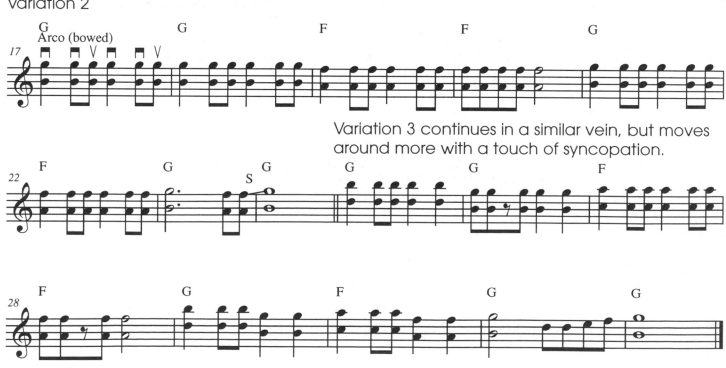

In this variation many upper neighbor notes embellish the basic melody.

LITTLE MAGGIE (Variation 4)

Variation 5 introduces some chromatic lower neighbor notes.

Variation 6 adds even more motion. Because the technical demands are pretty difficult, start slowly and gradually work your way up to speed.

The final variation moves into higher positions. Here again, start slowly and gradually work up to speed.

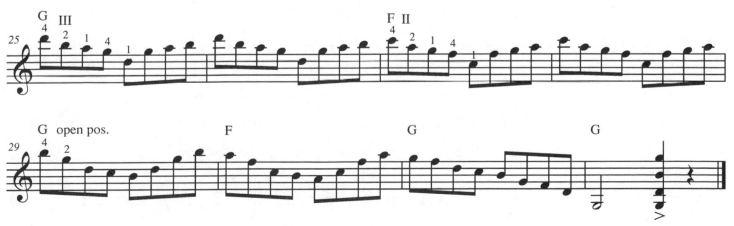

"John Hardy" is one of the many songs that tells the story of a desperado. It is written in a transposed Mixolydian mode. As you have learned, the Mixolydian mode consists of the notes G A B C D E F G. When transposed up a fifth (five notes) these notes become D E F# G A B C D, the same notes as the G major scale, but with a "home base" of D, not G. First learn the basic melody, then try the variations on the following pages. The G sus4 chord is new. It consists of the notes G C D.

JOHN HARDY (basic melody)

Variation 1 adds harmony notes both above and below the melody.

In measures 35, 37, and 39 slide up to the F# on the D string while playing the A string open.

**JOHN HARDY (Variation 2)** Here we add more eighth notes, neighbor notes and other embellishments you've learned.

Our last variation on "John Hardy" takes the melody up an octave into the 3rd position. It also includes various embellishments. Taking the melody up an octave puts it in a brighter, more brilliant sounding range. It's a good technique to use on your last chorus, building to an exciting finish to your improvisations.

# Bluegrass (concluded)

Our final selection is an old murder ballad which has become a Bluegrass standard. It is written in the key of A, which means that F, C, and G are always sharped unless there's a natural in front of the note. The chords used are A=A C♯ E, E7=E G♯ B D, A7=A C♯ E G and D=D F♯ A. Play the basic melody in cut time (two beats per measure).

BANKS OF THE OHIO (basic melody)

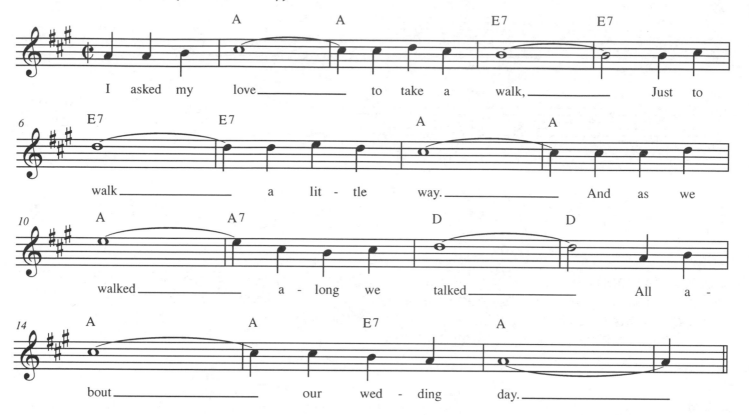

Our first variation harmonizes the melody with notes that are usually a third or sixth below.

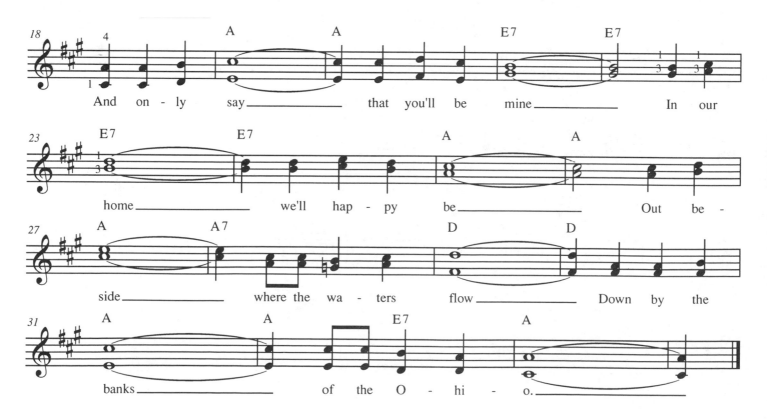

62

Our second variation makes use of a device called a **pedal point**. A pedal point is a note that is repeated along with a melody note throughout a section of a tune. The pedal point can be repeated even when it isn't part of the chord. Pedal points can be played above or below a melody. In this arrangement the note E is the pedal point. It's always above the melody, but since E is an open string, it doesn't pose any serious fingering problems.

BANKS OF THE OHIO (variation 2)

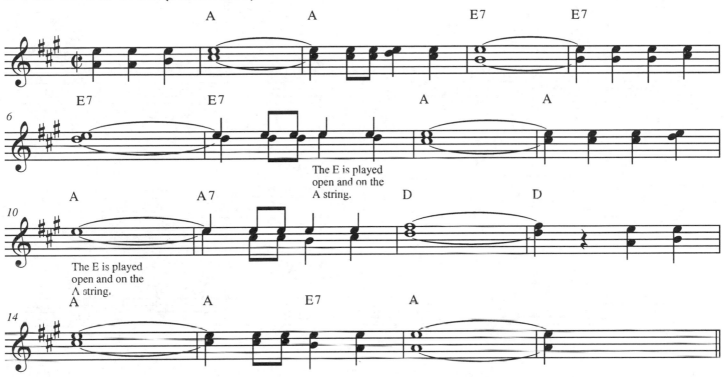

The eighth note triplet is a group of three eighth notes played in the time of two eighth notes, that is, one beat. This variation combines eighth note triplets with the pedal point from above.

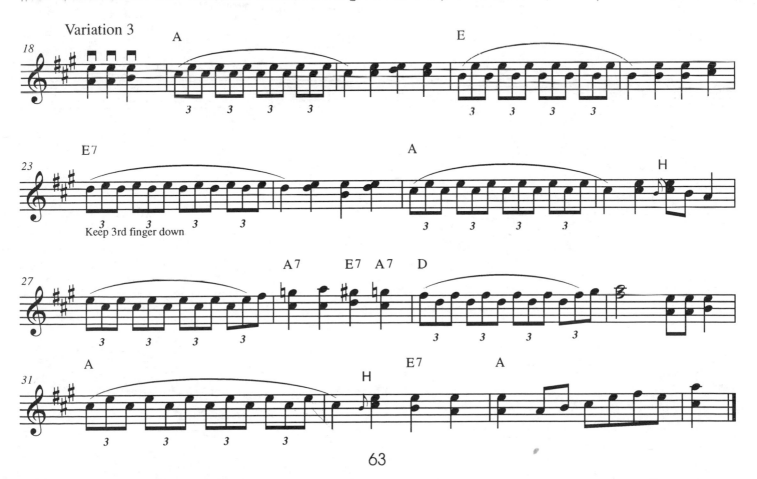

63

# Cajun Music

The Cajuns were French colonists who were exiled from Acadia during wars with the British in the 18th century. The word "Cajun" itself is a corruption of "Acadian." Now living in southern Louisiana, the Cajuns have developed a unique sound, an interesting blend of country fiddle with lots of slides and swoops (all sung in an 18th century French dialect). This piece is in two eight-bar sections, each of which is repeated. First learn the melody, then we'll add the "color" notes.

PARDON MY FRENCH (basic melody)

Track 12

Variation 1 makes extensive use of slides and neighbor notes

## PARDON MY FRENCH (variation 2)

The legendary Cajun fiddle player Doug Kershaw often used a variation like this one to add excitement to his performance. Pick two notes out of the chord and play them very rhythmically with down and up bowing. Just as a reminder: G=G B D; C=C E G; D7=D F♯ A C.

Our final variation moves into the higher register and, as usual in Cajun music, makes extensive use of slides.

Now add slides and grace notes where it sounds good to you.

# Irish Music

Many Irish tunes are in rapid 6/8 time. Count in two groups of three 8th notes, with the 1st and 4th beats getting the accent: **1** 2 3 **4** 5 6. The first example is an old dance tune sometimes used for the Virginia reel.

THE IRISH WASHERWOMAN (basic melody)

Track 13

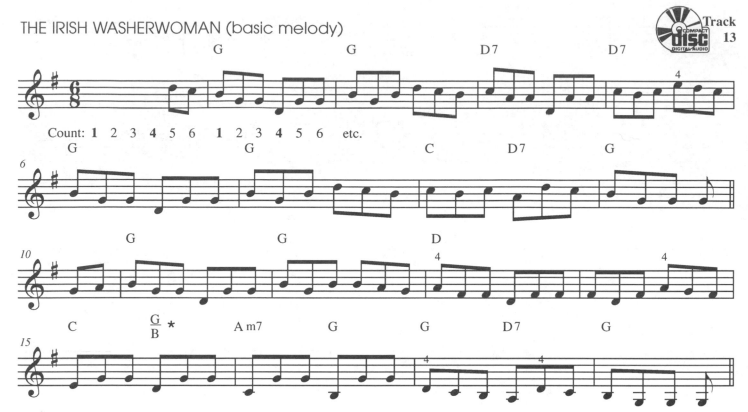

Although improvisations usually involve adding notes, sometimes a good effect can be obtained by simplifying a melody and reducing it to its essential notes. This is especially effective when dealing with a very busy melody like "The Irish Washerwoman." Notice how this variation outlines the melody, but with fewer notes. We have also moved part 2 of the song up an octave to put it in a brighter register.

Variation 1

\* $\frac{G}{B}$ means a G chord with B in the bass.

Irish jigs are often played at a medium tempo. One of their characteristics is the dotted 8th/16th rhythm which gives the jig a skipping, joyous feel. This jig is in the key of A minor. The chords are: Am=A C E; Dm=D F A; E7=E G# B D.

STRAIGHT JIG (basic melody)

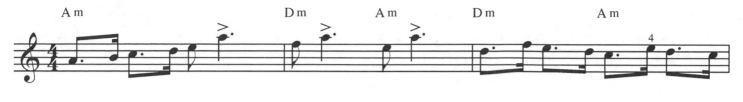

Our first variation adds an eighth note triplet figure to the basic rhythm. This is another typical jig rhythm.
Variation 1

Our next variation consists of a steady stream of 8th note triplets. Because this figure occurs over and over again, the "3" over each group is omitted. But notice that the melody is still recognizable.

STRAIGHT JIG (variation 2)

Our final variation steps up the rhythm to 16th notes. As usual, start slowly and gradually work your way up to tempo (about 96 beats per minute).
Variation 3

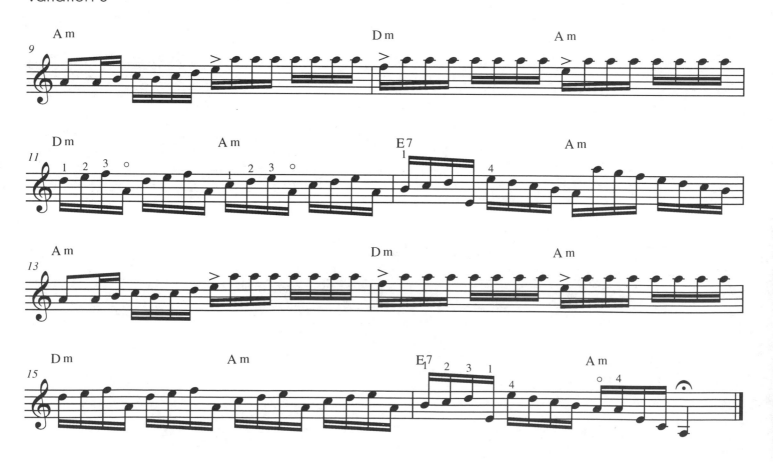

Although many Irish tunes are spirited romps in 6/8 or 4/4, Celtic music is also full of many beautiful ballads, often with a sad or nostalgic feeling. This song has been described as the most beautiful melody ever written. First learn the basic melody, then the variation on it.

DANNY BOY (Londonderry Air)

Melody: Traditional
Words: Fred Weatherly

But when ye come and all the flow'rs are dying,
If I am dead, as dead I well may be,
Ye'll come and find the place where I am lying
And kneel and say an Ave* there for me.

And I shall hear, though soft you tread above me
And all my grave will warmer, sweeter be,
For you will bend and tell me that you love me,
And I shall sleep in peace until you come to me.

pronounced: Ah-vay

Our variation makes use of full chords. Since the violin really can't play more than two notes at a time, the other notes of the chord are written as grace notes to be bowed just before the melody note. The harmony makes use of some chords that you may not have seen before: G/B means a G chord with B as the lowest note, B D G; Em7 (say: E minor seventh)= E G B D; Em=E G B; Cm=C E♭ G.
Play this song very slowly, and don't be too strict with the tempo.

DANNY BOY (variation)

# American Folk Music

Like America itself, American folk music comes from many sources. Since the majority of the early settlers came from the British Isles, many of our most beautiful songs come from that culture. Although the definitive version of "Wildwood Flower" was recorded by The Carter Family in the 1920s, the original source is lost in history. Notice that the melody is based on a C major hexachord (six-note scale), C D E F G A; that is, just like the C major scale but avoiding the leading tone B.

WILDWOOD FLOWER (basic melody)

Track 14

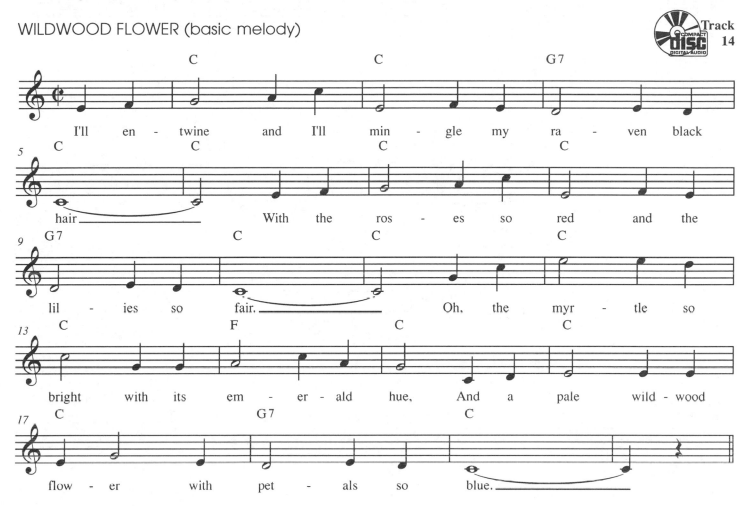

Variation 1 adds harmony notes mostly above the melody. Lower neighbors are also used, but this variations sticks fairly close to the basic melody.

The final variation departs from the melody. It also goes a little higher on the fingerboard to ease the fingering.

Many folk songs are in 3/4 time such as this typical example:

SWEET BETSY FROM PIKE (basic melody)

Variation 1 combines runs of 8th notes with double stops. The melody, though somewhat disguised, can still be recognized.

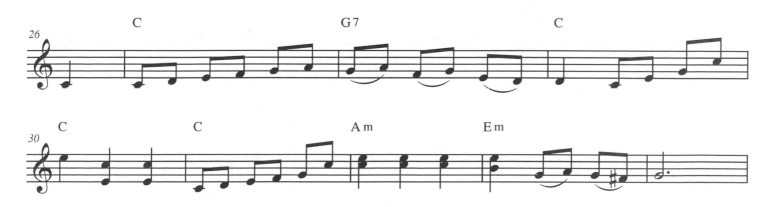

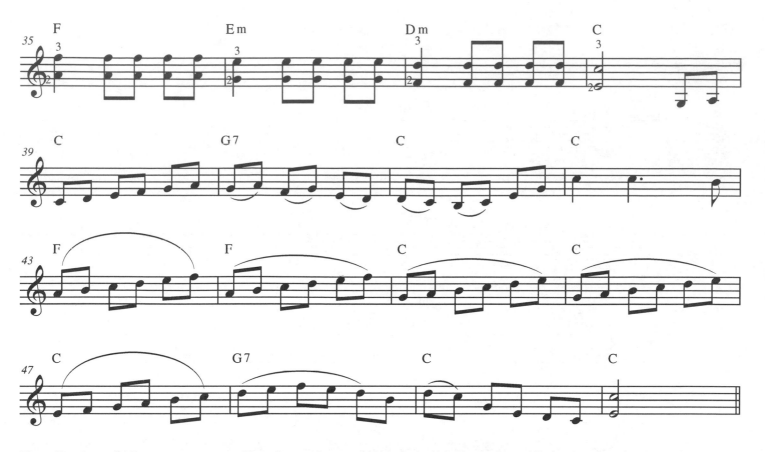

The final variation moves up the fingerboard. Watch the bowing, it's important.

For our last example of American folk music we've chosen a lively dance tune from the Ozark Mountains. As is often the case in square dance tunes, the song is notated in 2/4. Count the rhythms as "1 and 2 and" and keep a brisk tempo going.

FLY AROUND, MY PRETTY LITTLE MISS (basic melody)

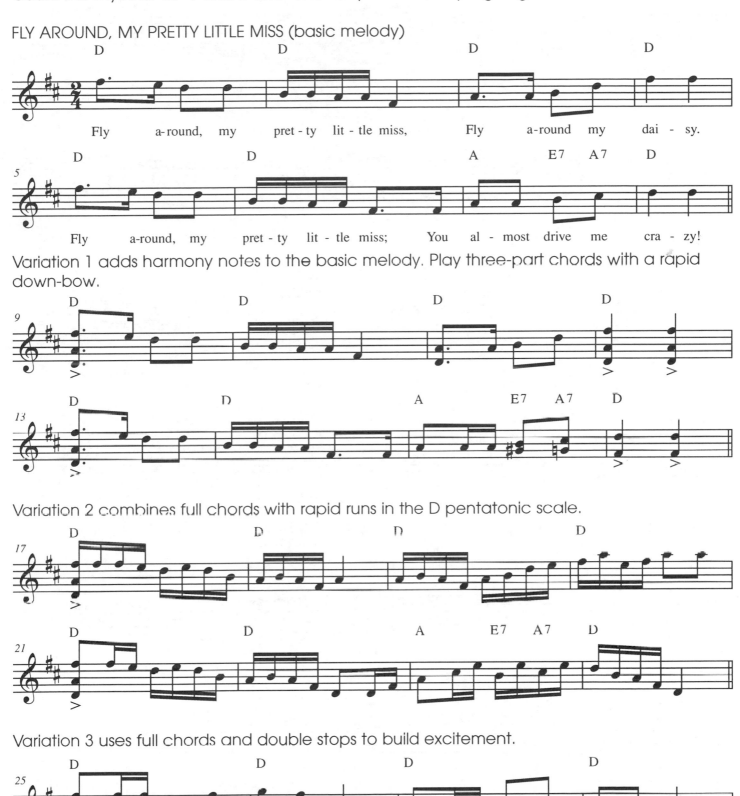

Variation 1 adds harmony notes to the basic melody. Play three-part chords with a rapid down-bow.

Variation 2 combines full chords with rapid runs in the D pentatonic scale.

Variation 3 uses full chords and double stops to build excitement.

Variation 4 uses double stops and runs in the D major scale.

Variation 5 is more rhythmic and exciting

Variation 6 restates the melody, sliding up to the F♯ on the A string.

Coda: After your final variation it's often very effective to add a short phrase to sort of sum up the piece as in the four measures below.

# Ragtime

Some time after the Civil War African-American pianists living in the Southwest started playing in a syncopated style they called "ragging the time." This was soon shortened to "ragtime," and the music became an international craze. Although improvisation is not a particularly important part of ragtime, two examples will show you a few possibilities. The first tune dates from 1909 and contains a chromatic passage that many violin players find troublesome to play (measures 7 and 8). You can use whichever fingering we've given. Notice the extensive use of chromatic neighbor notes in the melody itself.

TEMPTATION RAG(original melody)

Track 15    Henry Lodge

* B diminished = B D F A♭ (G♯)

77

As we previously stated, improvisation is not a big part of ragtime. Nevertheless, you can enhance what you play by adding chord tones, grace notes, and especially filling in dead spots in the melody, for example empty downbeats such as measures 21, 23, 29–31. But our advice is to stick closely to the melody.

TEMPTATION RAG (variation)                                                    Henry Lodge

# White Gospel

White gospel is a very emotional type of music, often with a mournful quality, especially popular in the South. All the techniques you have applied to folk and Bluegrass may be used, especially slides and pentatonic scales. Rhythmically, the 1st and 3rd beats of the measure are accented as opposed to Black gospel (which see).

Track 16

WILL THE CIRCLE BE UNBROKEN (basic melody)

WILL THE CIRCLE BE UNBROKEN (Variation)

Suggestion: Play the eighth notes swing style: long short long short

79

# Black Gospel

Like White gospel, Black gospel is a highly emotional music with a strong rhythmic feel. Unlike White gospel, however, the accents fall on the 2nd and 4th beats of the measure. This famous gospel song is based on an E minor pentatonic scale: E G A B D. Syncopation is an important feature of this music. Count carefully as indicated.

WADE IN THE WATER (basic melody)

This variation should be played with a swing feel. The eighth notes are played long short long short.

# The Blues

Modern blues are usually based on a 12-bar series of chords called "the blues progression." Musicians sometimes use Roman numerals to refer to chords in a key. For example in the key of C the I chord is C major, the IV is F major, and the V7 chord is G7. The basic blues progression consists of one measure each of the following chords: I I I I7 IV7 IV7 I I V7 V7 I I(V7). Of course, there are hundreds of variations on this basic progression, but the above sequence will be useful in most situations.

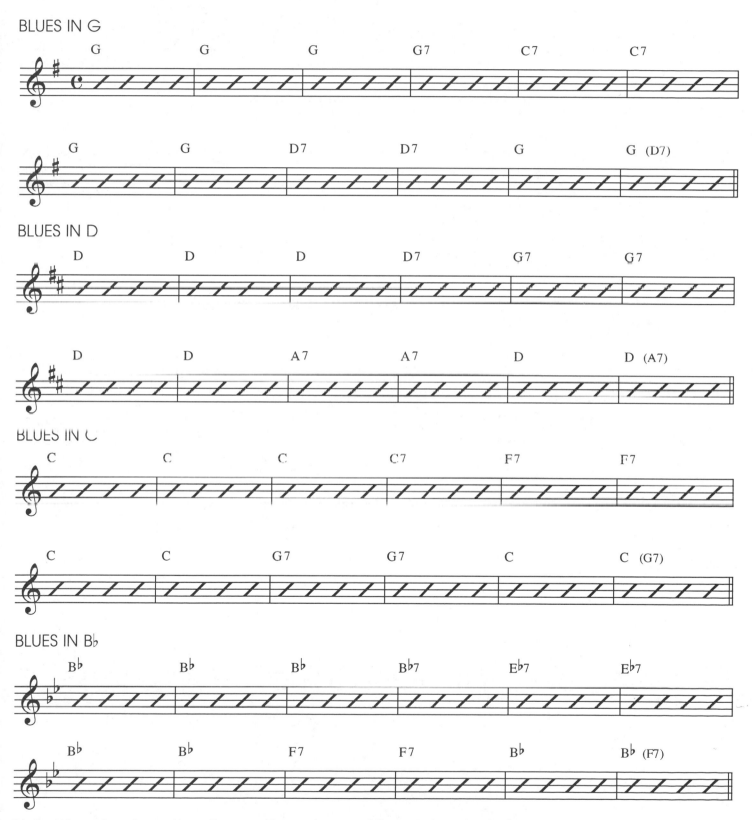

Note: If you've forgotten the spelling of any of these chords check back to page 46.

The blues scale is a special scale that is often used with the blues progression. One of the things that makes the blues so interesting is the tension between the notes in the blues scale with the notes in the accompanying chords. For example, the G blues scale uses a B♭ while the accompanying chord (G7) uses a B natural. The best thing about blues scales is that any note you play will sound good against the chords. Here are six blues scales in the most used keys.

THE G BLUES SCALE

Notice the flatted 3rd, the flatted 7th, and the 5th, which can be flat or natural.

THE D BLUES SCALE

THE A BLUES SCALE

THE C BLUES SCALE

THE E BLUES SCALE

THE B♭ BLUES SCALE

This typical moderate blues illustrates various techniques used with this type of music. All the grace notes are played as slides with the same finger. Also notice that although the basic melody mostly uses the G major scale, the variations stick to the G blues scale.

BLUES IN G (first chorus)
Swing feel: 8th notes played long-short

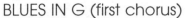

The second chorus makes extensive use of the flatted third (B♭) and repeats a two-bar riff over the various chord changes.

The third chorus is pure G blues scale with triplets adding motion and excitement.

83

One of the ways the blues progression is used is below. The predominant feel is the dotted 8th/16th note figure; think: hump-ty, dump-ty, hump-ty, dump-ty, for the right groove.

PIZZICATO BOOGIE (basic melody)

This piece and variations can also be played with down and up bows.

Note: the IV7 is sometimes substituted for the V7 here.

This sequence of chords is called a "turnaround." It prepares for the next chorus.

2nd chorus

Strum across three strings like a guitar

The third chorus of "Pizzicato Boogie" uses three-part chords like a guitar might play them. Strum across the strings with your fingernail and remember to keep the swing feel for the eighth notes (long short long short). This type of rhythmic playing of chords can be very effective especially if your fiddle is amplified.

PIZZICATO BOOGIE (3rd chorus)

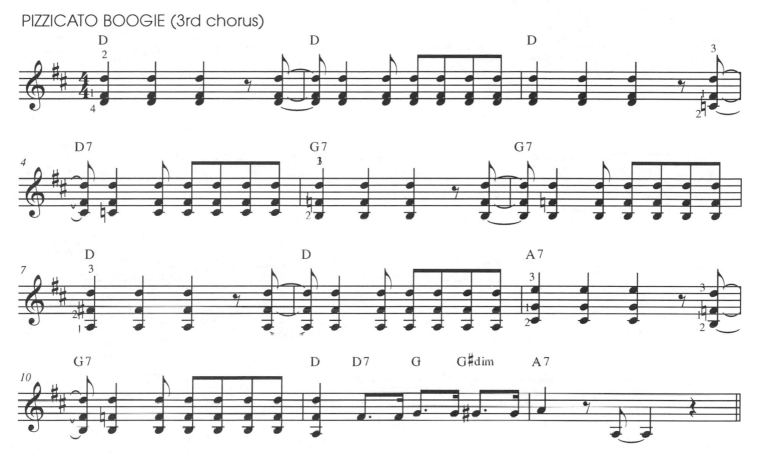

The fourth and final chorus makes use of an effect called **pitch bending**. Play the F natural as usual. Then roll the finger slightly upward so that the pitch rises by about a quarter tone (not quite to F#). Then roll back to the F natural. This is a very common effect on the blues.

Arco (with the bow)

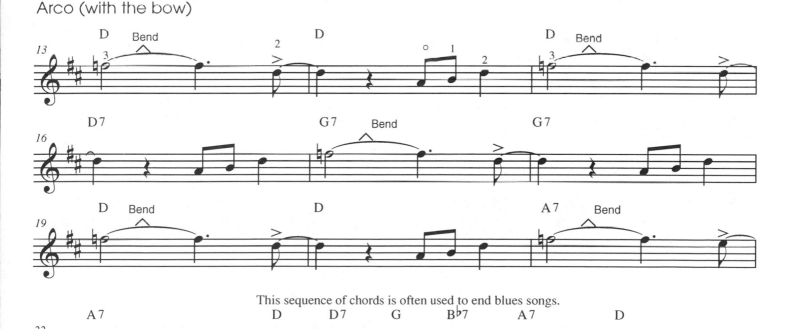

The blues progression has also been used in rock. The feel here is the "straight" feel. That is, all 8th notes are played equally. Count 1 & 2 & 3 & 4 &. Use all down bows for a more hard-driving sound.

ROCKIN' THE BLUES (basic version)

You can create your own rock blues using the version above as a model. Here are a few suggestions:

In the key of G the three basic chords are G, C, and D7. Here are some patterns you can adapt to the blues progression:

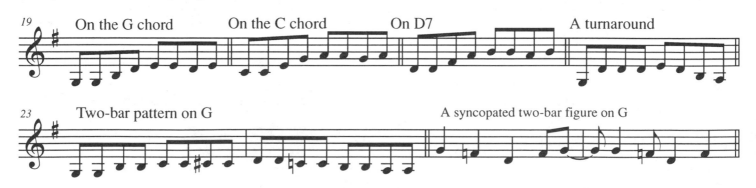

A very full-sounding pattern that can be adapted to any chord.

# Odd Meters

So far in this book we have dealt with meters that are common in Western popular music, 2/4, 3/4, 6/8, and especially 4/4 and cut time. In many parts of the world it's common to play music in odd meters like 5/4 or 7/8. Odd meters are interesting because they produce asymmetrical measures. In 4/4 we hear two halves of a measure, each like a measure of 2/4. In 6/8, the two halves contain three 8th notes each. But in an odd meter such as 5/4, one half of the measure contains three quarter notes; the other half only two.

The key to counting odd meters is to break them down into smaller units. For example, one measure of 5/4 can be thought of as a measure of 3/4 followed by a measure of 2/4. Or, one measure of 2/4 followed by a measure of 3/4. Example 84A.1

Similarly, a measure of 7/8 is usually counted as a measure of 3/8 followed by a measure of 2/4 (4/8) although it can be counted 2/8+3/8+2/8 or 2/4+3/8. The Greeks are particularly fond of 7/8, and their folk music is full of examples of this meter. Example 84A.2

Although in Western music 9/8 is usually counted as three groups of three 8th notes, in Greece and the near East it is often played as 2/8+2/8+2/8+3/8. Example 84A.3

Here's how to count many odd meters, although we wish to stress that other combinations are possible, and that the ones here are only the most common ways of counting them.

5/2, 5/4, or 5/8: 3+2 or 2+3. Counting in an even five beats to the measure is rare but can be found in the slow movement of Tschaikovsky's 4th symphony. 5/2 is very unusual, but was used in a few spots by Samuel Barber in his famous "Adagio for Strings."

6/4 or 6/8: Almost always counted in two groups of three, but listen to the song "America" from Leonard Bernstein's "West Side Story" for 6/8 counted alternately in two groups of three followed by three groups of two.

7/4 or 7/8: see above

9/8: see above

10/8: Usually counted 3+2+2+3. Very common in Romanian folk music.

11/8: 3+2+3+3, 3+3+3+2, or 3+2+2+2+2.

Even more elaborate rhythms are possible, but just remember to break them down into groups of 3 and 2.

In this example 5/4 is sometimes counted 3+2 and sometimes 2+3.

FIVE TIMES FOUR (basic melody)

Our variation uses similar notes in different registers. See if you can identify the 3+2 and 2+3 bars.

The next piece is in 7/8 counted **1** 2 3 **1** 2 **1** 2. The Bela of the title refers to the great 20th century Hungarian composer Bela Bartok who often used odd meters in his compositions.

THE OTHER BELA (basic melody)

Our first variation simplifies the melody

Variation 2 combines lower notes with upper chords to create an exciting rhythmic effect.

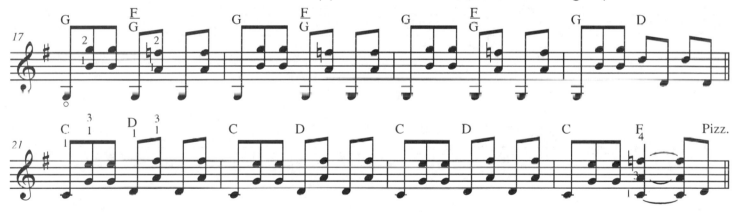

Variation 3 combines pizzicato with arco for an unusual improvisation.

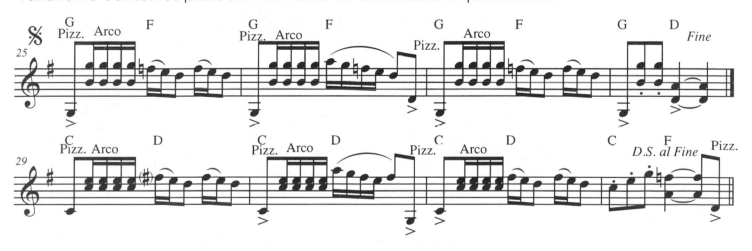

Although 9/8 time is usually counted in three groups of three 8th notes, the example below illustrates that other combinations are possible. This 9/8 is counted 1 2 1 2 1 2 1 2 3. Many Greek folk songs and dances are written in this meter. Here's an eight-bar tune and three variations on it.

ODYSSEY IN 9/8

Var. 1 Simplified version of melody.

Var. 2 Chords broken up rhythmically

Var. 3 A higher version all on the E string

# Exotic scales

Certain scales have such a distinctive sound that you can use them to suggest a particular mood or culture. Although it's beyond the scope of this book to give you all of them (there are hundreds!) we'll give you a taste of the most useful ones.

THE WHOLE TONE SCALE
as the name suggests, this scale has the interval of a whole tone (two half steps) between each scale tone. The whole tone scale is often used to suggest a dreamlike state, either in single notes or combined into double stops or chords.

WHOLE TONE SCALE ON D

WHOLE TONE SCALE ON E♭

A few things to remember about whole tone scales:

1. Because the scales have no real tonal center, the accidentals can be spelled with sharps or flats, depending on the surrounding music.

2. Because the scales consist only of whole steps (unlike major and minor scales which consist of half steps and whole steps) any note in the scale can serve as the key note.

3. The above two scales are the only possible whole tone scales.

WHERE TO USE THE WHOLE TONE SCALE

You won't find many places to use this scale unless you're into avant garde jazz or other cutting-edge sounds. If the accompanying chord belongs to one of the whole tone scales you can use improvisations from the scale. For example, if the accompanying chord is C+ (C augmented), the notes in the chord are C E G♯, all of which belong to the D whole tone scale. You can then use that scale to create your improv.

Suggestion: Make up your own improvisation based on one or both of the whole tone scales.

**A word of caution: Because of so many similar intervals (whole steps), the ear soon grows tired of this sound, so use it sparingly.**

# Klezmer music

Klezmer music developed in central Europe hundreds of years ago. Itinerant Jewish musicians wandered through the countryside playing their music for a bare subsistence. During the early period of klezmer they absorbed influences from traditional Hassidic tunes, Turkish, Hungarian, Romanian and other folk songs. When they came to America starting in about 1880, they were influenced by what they heard, and in the 1920s were strongly influenced by jazz. Today there is a great resurgence in klezmer music which is featured by such modern groups as "The Klezmatics" and "The Gypsy Kings."

One of the things that makes this music so interesting is the use of exotic scales, one of which is called "Misherabach." This scale resembles the Dorian mode, but has a raised fourth step. It is usually written with a key signature of no sharps or flats with the fourth step (G) sharped whenever it occurs.
MISHERABACH (the scale)

Track 19

CHOSEN KALLE MAZEL TOV

Jewish wedding song

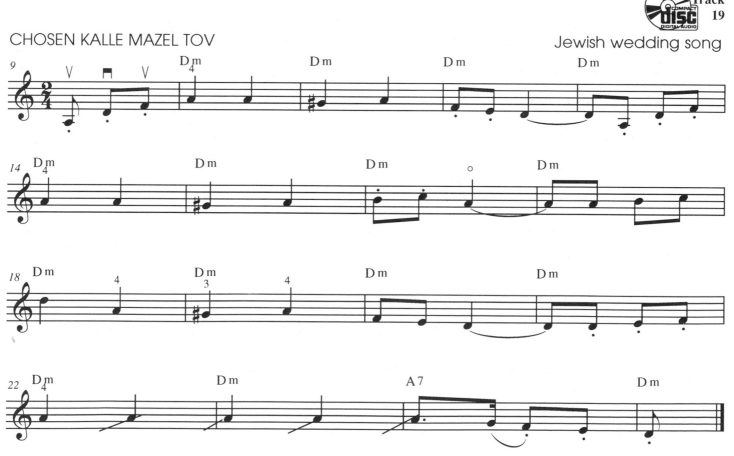

See next page for hints on improvisation.

These variations make use of typical devices of klezmer music: Grace notes, slides, and scale runs. Notice that all the added notes belong to the scale Misherabach.

CHOSEN KALLE MAZEL TOV (variation in upper octave)

Another variation, this time in the lower octave.

Many klezmer tunes are in the harmonic minor. However, you'll notice that in the first two sections of this famous tune the tonal center is actually D, not G. It's only in Part 3 that the song arrives at the G minor tonality. You may want to review section on harmonic minor scales.

HAVAH NAGILAH                                                      Traditional Jewish dance

The short trill ∿ is a very commonly used ornament in klezmer music. Here's a variation on "Havah Nagilah" that uses the short trill as well as other ornaments. We've also taken the melody up an octave for a more brilliant register.

HAVAH NAGILAH (variation)

Traditional Jewish dance

Note extended ending

95

# Exotic scales (cont.)

A scale called "Fraigish" is a popular one in klezmer music. It is also used in Greek music especially in the famous song "Misirlou" (popular with both Greek and Jewish audiences). It is based on D, usually written with a two sharp key signature with the rest of the accidentals written in where needed. Notice the curious mixture of sharps and flats in the same scale.

FRAIGISH or GREEK SCALE

GOODBYE TO PIRAEUS

Our variation adds typical ornaments to the basic melody.

96

Gypsies began to arrive in Europe in about the15th century. They brought with them a long tradition that incorporated many musical elements including some from North India, their ancestral home. Once in Europe they absorbed many elements from those musics, especially those from Spain and Hungary. This is one of the many exotic scales that Gypsies use in their folk music. It resembles a D harmonic minor scale, but with the fourth (G) raised a half step to G♯.

GYPSY SCALE

GYPSY FANTASY

This variation moves up the octave and adds a few ornaments.

Although many Gypsy songs have a slow, bittersweet quality like the one on the previous page, some are played at a much faster tempo. The scale is the same, but the cut time meter gives this song a bright, joyous sound.

AT THE GYPSY CARAVAN

Our variation uses many florid passages and trills typical of the Gypsy fiddling style. The final accelerando (speeding up) is also typical.

Although Scottish music generally sticks to ordinary major and minor scales, it often contains a rhythm rarely found elsewhere. The so-called "Scotch snap" is usually written as a 16th note followed by a dotted 8th. The dotted 8th gets the accent, so it's important not to let it slip onto the downbeat, as the whole effect of this rhythm is the accented up-beat.

HIGHLAND FLING                                                                 Scottish dance

Our variation uses a few ornaments and changes in register, but keeps the melody intact.

99

This Rumanian horra or circle dance uses the scale D E♭ F♯ G A B♭ C D. It is in the unusual meter of 3/8. Count in three, with the 8th note getting the beat.

1  &  2  &  3  &    Many of the ornaments are in the original. Some we have added.

This Palestinian folk song is in the Phrygian mode (see p.33) except for part 2 which is in the
key of G major. We've given you two different versions of each phrase, first the basic
melody, then a variation on it. This is a good plan to follow when playing a tune with a lot of
repetition.

ARTSA ALINU                                                              Palestinian folk song

The Japanese culture is one of the world's richest in terms of poetry, art, and music, so we can only scratch the surface here. One of the scales used in much of Japanese folk music is a pentatonic scale on D. It resembles a D natural minor scale but with the fourth step (G) and the seventh step (C) omitted.

JAPANESE PENTATONIC SCALE

Traditionally, Japanese melodies are not harmonized, but when playing Westernized versions it is not inappropriate to add chords as in the example below.

THE GEISHA'S LAMENT

The Chinese culture is one of the world's oldest. Much Chinese folk music is based on pentatonic scales. This example is in the D pentatonic scale: D E F♯ A B. Keep your variations to this scale, but chromatic embellishments may be used sparingly.

THE GOLDEN BELL

102

# Rock and Roll

The chord progression C Am Dm7(or F) G7—sometimes called the I VI II(or IV) V progression —is found in many 50s pop and rock songs including "Why Must I Be a Teenager in Love," "Heart and Soul," "26 Miles," "Blue Moon," and many others. First try this chord progression as single notes, then as two-part, and finally as three-part chords.

Here are a few variations on this four-bar progression:

Playing the chords in a triplet rhythm is typical of "doo-wop" ballads.

The same chords played as triplet arpeggios. (Arpeggios break up the chords into individual notes.)

In the key of G the I VI II V progression consists of: G=G B D; Em=E G B; Am7=A C E G or C=C E G; and D7=D F♯ A C. In these variations each chord is played for two beats only.

I VI II(IV) V PROGRESSION IN G (simple root tones)

Two-part chords

Three-part chords

Variations

The dotted quarter/eighth note rhythm.

With syncopation (accented off-beats)

A different syncopated figure with each chord played for four beats.

The same syncopation in two-part chords

Now try your own variations in C and G and in other common keys like F, D, A, and E.

# Rock and Roll (cont.)

The next tune is a 50s style rock song played at a pretty good clip. The melody is based on the I VI II V progression in the key of C and is eight measures long. Three variations follow.

BACK TO THE FIFTIES

Track 20

Variation 1 uses the same rhythms on different notes.

Variation 2 keeps the same feeling of syncopation, but adds more notes and a few embellishments.

Variation 3 features figures that start off the beat.

Count: 1 & 2 & 3 & 4 &

Our final versions of the I VI II V progression have a feel sometimes called "boogaloo." The 4/4 measures are felt as eight even beats to the bar; that is, each eighth note gets a beat. Famous records that have this feel are The Beatles' "Let It Be," and The BeeGees "Stayin' Alive."

# Disco

Disco became popular in the 70s, but seems destined to be around a long time. Disco features a lot of double-time (eighth note based) rhythms contrasted with much smoother, longer-held notes. The violin plays an important part in this kind of music, often punctuating the arrangement with falls (see p.15) glisses (long slides) and fast upward runs (sometimes called "sweeps"). This tune is a typical disco-styled arrangement based on only two chords: Cmaj7=C E G B and Dm7/G=D F A C over a G bass note.

DISCO DAZE

# Country and Folk Rock

The next piece is designed to suggest the feel of The Eagles' famous "Hotel California." You should be familiar with all the chords used, but we'll review them just the same: Am=A C E; E7=E G# B D; G=G B D; D=D F# A; F=F A C; A=A C# E.

NEVADA MOTELS (the basic chord progression (need not be played))

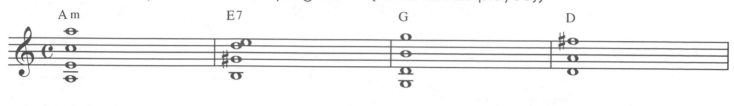

Basic melody

Variation 1 makes use of grace notes and trills but still suggests the melody.

Variation 2 ignores the melody and plays a 3+3+2 eighth note figure that suggests syncopation because some of the accents fall on the up beats.

# The A Tuning

Although the violin is ordinarily tuned G D A E, some country fiddlers like to use alternate tunings to get a different sound and, by making use of more open strings, make fingering easier. In the next country standard the G and D strings are each raised a whole step to A and E respectively. The fiddle is now tuned A E A E, allowing you to make use of the open lower A and E strings—a big advantage when playing in the key of A. However, don't forget that any note below middle A now has to be fingered a whole step lower than in normal tuning.

Ordinary tuning     The "A" tuning     Fingering for notes on the lower two strings

Track 21

RYE WHISKEY
(Notes with the stems going down are played on the low A and E strings)

Rye whiskey, rye whiskey,
Rye whiskey I crave.
If I don't have rye whiskey
I'll go to my grave

I eat when I'm hungry
And drink when I'm dry,
And if whiskey don't kill me
I'll live till I die.

Here's another traditional fiddle tune that works well in the A tuning. First, review the material about this tuning on page 109. The tune is written in two sections, each one being repeated. On the repeats we've added some possible embellishments and lower notes which make use of the re-tuned low A and E.

LOST INDIAN (Part 1, basic melody)

Part 1, variation

Part 2, basic melody

Part 2, variation

# The A tuning (cont.)

Our next song in the A tuning is the country standard "Sally Goodin'." It consists of four eight-bar sections. Make sure your fiddle is in A tuning: A E A E. Remember that notes with the stems going down are played on the lower strings which have been re-tuned.

SALLY GOODIN'

For our final example of the A tuning we have chosen a beautiful hymn. Because the original melody appears to be of Scottish origin, using the open low A and low E strings is particularly appropriate because it suggests the sound of bagpipes.

AMAZING GRACE
As the entire tune is played over an A/E pedal point, no real chords are used.

You may want to experiment with other tunings. Here are a few possibilities:

1. G tuning: Same as the A tuning a whole step lower. Use for the key of G.
2. D tuning: Use for the key of D. If the low D sounds too dull because the string is so slack, try using a viola low C string.
3. E major tuning. Use for the key of E.
4. E minor tuning. Use for the key of E minor.

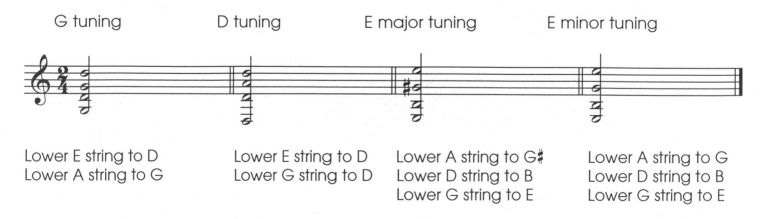

| G tuning | D tuning | E major tuning | E minor tuning |
|---|---|---|---|
| Lower E string to D | Lower E string to D | Lower A string to G♯ | Lower A string to G |
| Lower A string to G | Lower G string to D | Lower D string to B | Lower D string to B |
| | | Lower G string to E | Lower G string to E |

This concludes the musical portion of this book. On the next few pages you'll find lists of books and recordings that explore these and other aspects of modern violin playing.

## PLAYING WITH OTHER PEOPLE

If you find yourself playing in a group or even with one other player, say a guitarist, it's important to remember a few things that will make your experience (and the experience of your listeners) more enjoyable.

1. Make sure that you're in tune with the other instrument(s). Although some electronic keyboards can be tuned, most of them are tuned at the factory to the standard pitch of A=440 vibrations per second. Therefore, it's your responsibility to get in tune with the keyboard, not the other way around. If you don't have a keyboard in your group make sure that everyone tunes to the same source. There are reasonably priced electronic tuners on the market as well as tuning forks and pitch pipes that can be used for reliable tuning. Violin is a notoriously treacherous instrument to keep in tune, so do not neglect this important facet of ensemble playing.

2. Find people to play with who are sympathetic to your kind of music. Trying to play bluegrass fiddle with a jazz guitar player or a polka band accordion player is a recipe for chaos.

3. Although working out arrangements by ear and instinct can produce some fine music, this method can also be very time consuming. In our opinion it's better to start with at least a lead sheet for all the members of the group. A lead sheet contains the melody, chords, and words (if it has any) to a song. This way everybody starts out with the same basic knowledge about the song, especially the melody and chords. This still leaves plenty of room for creativity.

4. After you decide what you're going to play, choose a tempo that everyone in the group feels comfortable with. Better to play a slower tempo that sounds relaxed than one that's so fast that you sound like you're hanging on by your fingernails.

## PLANNING YOUR ARRANGEMENTS

It's important to pick a routine (a word musicians use to describe how a composition or arrangement is put together) and stick to it. Otherwise, embarassing things tend to happen like two people trying to solo at once or—worse yet—nobody playing the lead.

A sample routine for a song that has words might be:

Introduction (usually four or eight measures, often based on the last few measures of the song)
1st chorus–The melody played straight with few variations
2nd chorus–The melody sung by one or more members of the group
3rd chorus– Fiddle solo (improvised)
4th chorus–Second verse and chorus sung
5th chorus–Guitar solo (improvised)
6th chorus–Another sung verse and chorus
7th chorus–Another improvised verse and chorus by keyboard or mandolin
8th and 9th choruses–Ensemble instrumental gradually building to a big finish
Coda (anywhere from two to eight measures)

Along with your improvised solos, how you plan your arrangements is an important place to demonstrate your creativity. Use your planning as a springboard, not a straitjacket. If things are going well, expand the routine. For example, double the length of the solos. If you can't quite get it together, cut the arrangement short and try a different tune.

## DEVELOPING AN ORIGINAL STYLE

It's difficult and time-consuming to develop an original musical style. Improvising is part of the picture, but so is tone, rhythm, your individual sound on the violin, and how you plan your arrangements. It's difficult to define what makes someone develop an individual style. What seems to work for most players is to start out by emulating a musician whose playing they admire. Some people never get beyond mere imitation. Others take an admired player's style as a starting point and gradually begin to add their own touches until their own individuality emerges. In the long run you must follow your own musical instinct. If it sounds right to you...go with it!

# FIDDLE BOOKS OF INTEREST

Usher Abel: *Jazz Violin Solos* Mel Bay Publications, Inc. (with CD)

Allen: *Canadian Fiddle Tunes* Bernadol Pub. Co.

Paul Anastasio: *Swing Fiddle Tunes* Ridge Runner Video

Darol Anger: *Blues on the Fiddle* Homespun Tapes DVD

Aly Bain: *50 Fiddle Solos* (with CD) Music Sales

David Brody: *The Fiddler's Fakebook* Oak Publications

Kevin Burke: *Learn to Play Irish Fiddle* Homespun Tapes DVD

Mike Connolly and Dick Weissman: *Easy Fiddle Solos* Mel Bay Publications, Inc. (with CD)

Craig Duncan: *Fiddling Classics* (with CD) Mel Bay Publications, Inc.

Craig Duncan: *The Cajun Fiddle* (with CD) Mel Bay Publications, Inc.

Craig Duncan: *Top Fiddle Solos* (with CD) Mel Bay Publications, Inc.

Michael Doucet: *Learn to Play Real Cajun Fiddle* Book and CD Homespun Tapes

Tom Giland: *Favorite Swedish Fiddle Tunes* Mel Bay Publications, Inc.

Matt Glaser and Stephane Grapelli *Jazz Violin* Oak Publications

Deborah Greenblatt: *The Cajun Fiddle Tune Book* Centerstream Pub. (with CD)

Deborah Greenblatt: *The International Fiddler's Tune Book* Greenblatt and Seay Publications

Mary Ann Harbor: *Gypsy Violin* Mel Bay Publications, Inc. (with CD)

Brad Leftwich: *Learn to Play Old-Time Fiddle* Homespun Tapes DVD

No author listed: *Complete Fiddling Book (anthology)* Mel Bay Publications, Inc. (with CD)

Ken Perlman: *The Fiddle Music of Prince Edward Island* Mel Bay Publications, Inc. (with CD)

Stacy Phillips: *Easy Klezmer Tunes* Mel Bay Publications, Inc. (with CD)

Stacy Phillips: *Hot Licks for Bluegrass Fiddle* Oak Pub. (with CD)

Stacy Phillips: *Natalie McMaster's Cape Breton Island Fiddle* Mel Bay Publications, Inc. (with CD)

Mark O'Connor: *The Championship Years* Mel Bay Publications, Inc. (with CD)

Marion Thede: *The Fiddle Book* Oak Publications

Jay Ungar: *A Fiddler's Guide to Waltzes, Airs, and Melodies* Homespun Tapes DVD

Robin Williamson: *English, Welsh, Scottish, and Irish Fiddle Tapes* Oak Pub. (with CD)

# FIDDLE RECORDINGS OF INTEREST

Tom Anderson and Aly Bain: *The Silver Bowl: The Fiddle Music of Scotland* Topic Records

Kenny Baker and Bobby Hicks: *Darkness on the Delta* County (Note: Many Kenny Baker cuts on Bill Monroe recordings)

Byron Berline: *Live at the Music Hall* Double Stop

Louis Boudreault: *Old Time Fiddler of Chicoutimi, Quebec* Voyager Records

Gatemouth Brown: *Pressure Cooker* Alligator

Kevin Burke: Many recordings of Irish fiddle music on Green Linnet

Vassar Clements: *Grass Routes* Rounder

Michael Doucet: Many recordings of Cajun music, including his own band, *Beausoleil*

Johnny Gimble: *The Texas Fiddle Collection* CMH

Stefan Grapelli: Numerous recordings with legendary guitarist Django Reinhardt as "The Quintet of the Hot Club of France," as well as soloist with other musicians

Lorentz Hod: *Hardanger Fiddle* NOR Records

*Polish Mountain Fiddle* Yazoo Records

Gid Tanner and His Skillet Lickers: *A Corn Licker Still in Georgia* Voyager Records

Benny and Jerry Thomasson: *The Weiser Reunion* (Texas fiddle) Voyager CD

*Joe Thompson Family Tradition* (African-American string band music) Rounder

Various artists: *He Sure Do Pull Some Bow* Old Hat

Various artists: *Violin, Sing the Blues For Me* Old Hat

Joe Venuti: Great jazz fiddle player. Look for reissues with guitarist Eddie Lang

Bob Wills and His Texas Playboys: Classic Texas swing—many reissued recordings, especially on Rhino Records.


Note: Many country and Bluegrass fiddle recordings are available on County, Rounder, Sugar Hill, and Voyager Records.

# Dick Weissman

Dick Weissman is the co-author of six published books about music and the music business. The Folk Music Sourcebook, co-authored with Larry Sandberg, won the ASCAP Music Critics Award, and his recent book, Which Side Are You On? An Inside History of the Folk Music Revival in America, was a finalist for the 2006 Oregon Book Award in non-fiction writing. His other books include the Music Business; Career Opportunities & Self Defense (which was also translated into Japanese), Three Rivers Press, 3rd revised edition, 2003, a best seller on the Random House back list, Blues: the Basics, and Making A Living In Your Local Music Market, 3rd revised edition, 2006. He has also written over 45 published instructional manuals for banjo, guitar, and songwriting.

While living in Colorado he was an Associate Professor in the Music & Entertainment Industry Program at the University of Colorado at Denver. He currently resides in Portland, Oregon, and is adjunct instructor at the University of Oregon, the University of Denver and Portland Community College.

Dick has enjoyed a long career as a studio musician, record producer, songwriter, composer and performer. During the 1960s, he recorded for Capitol Records in the pop-folk group The Journeymen. His 2005 album, "Solo," is an exploration of the banjo and guitar in a variety of unusual contexts that he likes to call folk jazz.

For more information about Dick Weissman, or to listen to some of his music, go to his web site: www.dickweissman.com

# Dan Fox

It's likely that Dan Fox has written and sold more popular music books than any other author in recent times. His Reader's Digest songbooks (17 in all) have sold more than 10 million copies. The total approaches 20 million when you include his best-selling John Denver Songbook and Compleat Beatles (in collaboration with Milt Okun), as well as songbooks for Kenny Rogers; Crosby, Stills, Nash, and Young; Peter Paul and Mary; and dozens of other stars of rock, folk, and country.

Dan has also written many instruction books for guitar and mandolin, as well as "Write It Right," a guide for music arrangers and copyists, "The Rhythm Bible," with more than 1000 exercises for rock and jazz musicians; and many more. He has published arrangements and original compositions ranging from simple harmonica solos to complete works for concert bands.

In the classical field, clarinettist Arthur Miller has recorded Dan's "Suite for Clarinet and Piano." Dan has also arranged books of solos by world-class artists such as Richard Stoltzman and Sir James Galway.

Dan's publishers include Mel Bay, Warner Bros. Music (where he was once editor-in-chief), Hal Leonard, Carl Fischer (where he was interim editor), Theodore Presser, and Alfred Publishing Co. He has also published "In and Out the Window" and "A Treasury of Children's Songs," highly successful children's songbooks for New York's prestigious Metropolitan Museum of Art.

Dan holds bachelor's and master's degrees in composition from the Manhattan School of Music where he was a scholarship student. He is married to artist June Fox. They have three children and seven grandchildren and divide their time between the west coast of Florida and the mountains of western North Carolina.